Be Dazzled!

GAIL BIRD

YAZZIE JOHNSON

MAYNARD WHITE OWL LAVADOUR

DIANA F. PARDUE

MASTERWORKS OF

JEWELRY AND

BEADWORK FROM

THE HEARD MUSEUM

PUBLISHED BY THE HEARD MUSEUM

PHOENIX, ARIZONA

©2002 BY THE HEARD MUSEUM
ALL RIGHTS RESERVED

ISBN 0-934351-65-1

DESIGN BY CAROL HARALSON
PHOTOS BY CRAIG SMITH
COPYEDITED BY JULIET MARTIN AND REBECCA STENHOLM
COORDINATED BY LISA MACCOLLUM

PRINTED IN CHINA

DISTRIBUTED BY
MUSEUM OF NEW MEXICO PRESS, SANTA FE

Library of Congress Cataloging-in-Publication Data

Be dazzled! : masterworks of jewelry and beadwork from
the Heard Museum / by Gail Bird ... [et al.].
     p. cm.
   ISBN 0-934351-65-1
       1. Indians of North America—Jewelry—
   Exhibitions. 2. Indians of North America—
   Jewelry—Southwest, New—Exhibitions.
   3. Indian beadwork—North America—
   Exhibitions. 4. Heard Museum—Catalogs.
   I. Bird, Gail, 1949- . II. Heard Museum.

   E98J48 B4 2002
   746.5'089'97078—dc21
                                    2001051966

Be Dazzled! is published through the generous support
of The Theodore Dubin Foundation. Funding for the
Masterworks series of publications was provided by the
Dr. and Mrs. Dean Nichols Publications Fund. This pub-
lication was produced in conjunction with the second
exhibit in the Masterworks series, Be Dazzled!
Masterworks of Jewelry and Beadwork from the Heard
Museum, sponsored by SRP, Bank of America and Joel
and Lila Harnett.

Exhibit dates at the Heard Museum:
March 23 to October 6, 2002

PHOTOGRAPHS:

Front cover, clockwise: Caddo brooch, early 1900s. 2 x .5. German silver. Heard Museum purchase, NA-PL-MS-J-2; Leekya Deyuse, Zuni, 1889-1966. Inlaid shell, 1930s-1950s. 1 x 3.2. Spondylous shell, turquoise, jet, shell. Gift of C.G. Wallace, NA-SW-ZU-J-66; Charles Bitsuie, Navajo. Button, 1933. 1.62 x .5. Silver. Gift of C.G. Wallace, NA-SW-NA-J-267; Navajo canteen, 1920-1940. 4 x 3 x 1.25. Silver. Fred Harvey Fine Arts Collection, 594S.

Back cover: Detail. Mackenzie River moss bag (cradle cover), late 1800s. 20 x 9. Velvet, glass beads, faceted steel beads, thread, canvas, leather. Gift of Florence D. Bartlett, NA-NE-CR-Q-108.

Title page: Teri Greeves, Kiowa/Comanche, b. 1970. Beaded sneakers, 1999. 16.5 x 12.5 x 4.25, Commercial canvas shoes, faceted glass beads and brass beads, thread. Heard Museum purchase, 3868-1A, B. Beadworkers adapt with time and use whatever is around them. They will bead almost anything, even tennis shoes and roller skates. — *Maynard White Owl Lavadour*

Contents page: Navajo belt, early 1900s. 36.5 x 3.38. Silver, leather. Fred Harvey Fine Arts Collection, 1051S. This is an early belt, as evidenced by the diamond slots used to thread the leather through to connect the belt and the tiny little bridle buckle. The conchos, probably coin silver, are more important than the buckle. Such belts are very heavy. To be worn comfortably, they are usually backed with leather around the conchos. On this belt, the leather backing is cut to the exact same dimensions as the con-chos, including their serrated edges. The silversmith used his stamps to vary the designs on the fourth and the fifth conchos interestingly. The stamp designs appear as tiny dots. — *Gail Bird and Yazzie Johnson*

Dimensions are given in inches, height preceding width.

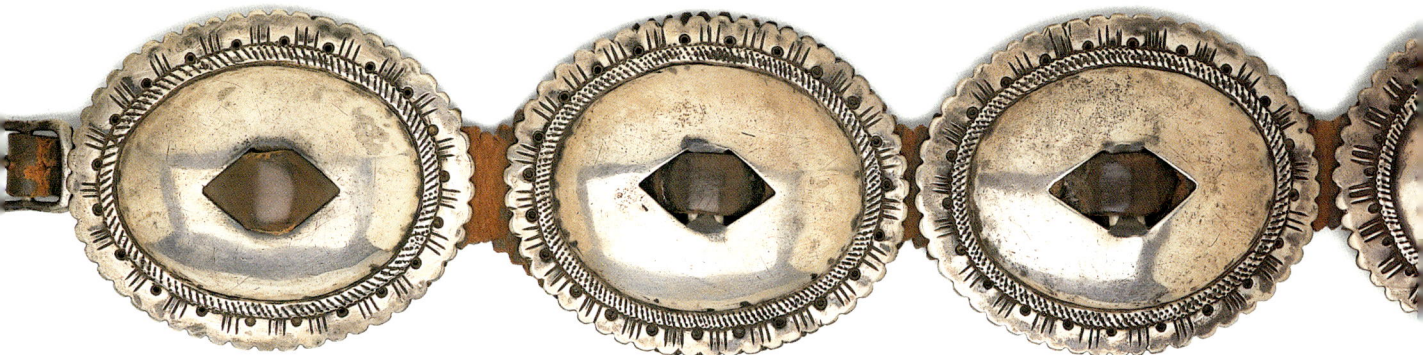

BE DAZZLED! A LITTLE HISTORY

DIANA F. PARDUE

KENNETH BEGAY
Navajo, 1913-1977
Pin, c. 1960

2.88. Silver. Estate of Carolann
Smurthwaite, NA-SW-NA-J-713.

WHEN the Heard Museum decided to undertake its Masterworks series the staff was excited about the opportunity to collaborate with guest curators, talented artists who would select and comment on works from the Heard's collection. This, the second in the series, was originally conceived to feature items of adornment. As collection strengths were reviewed by the project team, it became evident that the jewelry and beadwork collections were especially rich in examples of masterworks.

Immediately, the staff thought of Gail Bird, Santo Domingo/Laguna, and Yazzie Johnson, Navajo, as guest curators for jewelry, and Maynard White Owl Lavadour, Cayuse/Nez Perce, to curate beadwork. These artists have a long history of working with the museum on exhibits and programs. All are accomplished at their respective arts, and all have a great appreciation for cultural history.

GAIL BIRD AND YAZZIE JOHNSON are known not only for their creative and technically skilled jewelry but also for their extensive research in the history of the art form among Native Americans. They are also known for groundbreaking innovations incorporating new materials and designs. Some of their works are whimsical and fun—paying homage to cats, dogs and dinosaurs—while others, such as the pearl necklaces they create, are formal and elegant. All are creatively designed and beautifully crafted.

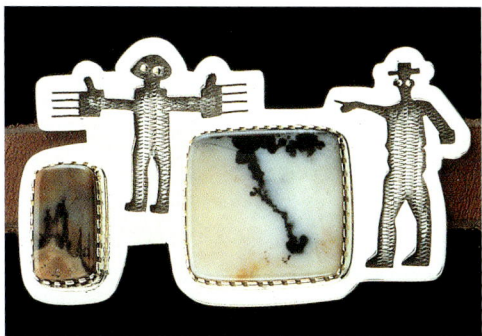

GAIL BIRD AND YAZZIE JOHNSON
Santo Domingo/Laguna, b. 1949
and Navajo, b. 1946
Route 66 tourism belt, 1995
45 x 1.75. Silver, gold, picture jasper, agates, turquoise, coral, petrified wood, Yowah opal, lapis lazuli, dendrites, spectrolite. Heard Museum purchase, 3578-1.

Bird and Johnson are self-taught artists who began creating jewelry in the mid-1970s. Early in their careers, they were recognized with awards at the Santa Fe Indian Market and a fellowship sponsored by the Southwestern Association of Indian Arts. They used the funds to study historic jewelry and to explore petroglyphs throughout the Four Corners region of the Southwest. Inspired by the many amazing uses of natural materials they saw in the work of early jewelers, they began to introduce a wide variety of natural stones into their own work.

Through the course of the research, Bird developed a slide lecture that illustrated the history of Southwestern jewelry making as well as the inspiration for much of the jewelry. She juxtaposed photographs of historic and contemporary jewelry with images of the landscape. In the late 1980s, museum members and staff had opportunities to attend Bird's slide lectures offered at seminars organized by Martha Streuver for the Crow Canyon Archaeological Center based in Cortez, Colorado. Through these lectures, one acquired not only a sense of the rich heritage of Southwestern jewelry but also the relationship of artists to the environment and to their respective homelands.

In 1994, Bird and Johnson agreed to work with the Heard in planning the exhibition *Inventing the Southwest: The Fred Harvey Company and Native American Art* through a review of the Fred Harvey Company Collection of jewelry at the museum. Their review of approximately 700 silver and turquoise items collected by the Harvey Company revealed a diverse collection including important early works that are simple and elegant in both shape and design. Also represented are many "one-of-a-kind" jewelry items, expressed particularly in the several hundred bracelets given to the museum by the Harvey Company. When the intensive survey ended, Bird and Johnson had a thorough view of the composition of the collection. The Heard selected fifty examples for the *Inventing the Southwest* exhibit, paying attention to Bird and Johnson's determination of superior works.

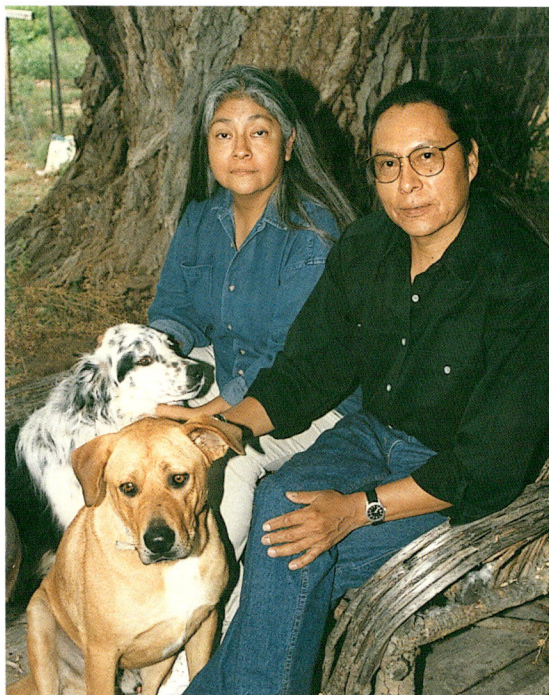

Photo by Gregory Lonewolf, 1995

MAYNARD WHITE OWL LAVADOUR
Cayuse/Nez Perce, b. 1960
Girl's dress, 1989
29 x 26.5. Pendleton wool, glass beads, buckskin, thread.
Heard Museum purchase from the exhibit *Native Art to Wear*, 3199-1A, B.

Although the exhibit gave a historic account of the Harvey Company and the Native artists involved with it, it also sought to convey that Native arts are vital and thriving, a tenet that is at the heart of the Heard Museum's mission. The exhibit featured works by descendants of artists who had worked for the Harvey Company as well as a smaller number of contemporary works selected to illustrate how early tourist pieces began an art market that today embraces outstanding artworks. To complement older pieces, the Heard wanted to purchase a belt by

This is a traditional dress for a little girl based on the design of buckskin dresses. The design represents mountains, and the diamonds at the front and back neck openings represent the tail of a deer.

——MAYNARD WHITE OWL LAVADOUR

Bird and Johnson. Then-director Martin Sullivan set out to do just that in August 1995 at the Santa Fe Indian Market, the only venue for which Bird and Johnson annually make a belt. The theme of the belt was unknown—it was to be revealed, as was the custom, for the first time only at the beginning of the annual market. The belts are thematic in nature and exquisite in execution. They incorporate a plethora of stones such as picture jasper, agates and others selected for the stones' pictorial nature and the way they enhance the story "told" in the silver and gold belts. Sullivan arrived at Bird and Johnson's booth on the plaza in Santa Fe on Saturday at six o'clock in the morning and found that he was third in the line of aspiring buyers. To Sullivan's surprise, the belt depicted a Route 66 theme that perfectly connected with the role of the Harvey Company in developing Southwestern tourism almost 100 years before. Fortunately for the museum, buyers one and two on the list selected other items, making the belt available to the museum. Interest in Bird and Johnson's work continues, as evidenced by the number of people that congregate at their booth each year at the Santa Fe Indian Market.

In 1997, Bird and Johnson were again associated with the museum when their jewelry was featured along with that of thirty-seven other jewelers in the exhibit *The Cutting Edge: Contemporary Southwestern Jewelry and Metalwork.* The slide lectures staff members had seen Bird give a decade before had an impact on the exhibit presentation. Expansive photo murals of the Southwestern landscape by photographers Jerry Jacka and Owen Seumptewa, Hopi, covered the exhibit walls above the cases filled with jewelry. The photographs showed some of the sources of inspiration for the diverse jewelry included in the exhibit.

Bird and Johnson brought more than twenty-five years of research, study, design and creation of jewelry to the selection of works for *Be Dazzled!* Many of their selections have delicate but carefully crafted features. Their review of the 3,000 items in the storage vault resulted in a selection of approximately 150 works for the exhibit.

MAYNARD WHITE OWL LAVADOUR'S connections to the museum have followed a course similar to that of Bird and Johnson. Lavadour brings to the Masterworks project a lifetime of admiration for and study of beadwork in addition to years of making beaded works. He spent much of his childhood with his two grandmothers, who taught him to bead while teaching him about Northwest Plateau people and culture. Lavadour recalls learning about colors and patterns as well as the history of objects. Through the years, he has received many awards at the Santa Fe Indian Market, the Heard Museum Guild Indian Fair & Market and other events.

The Heard Museum initially featured Lavadour's beadwork in 1987 in an exhibit titled *Native Art to Wear,* in some respects a predecessor to *Be Dazzled!* Two items made by Lavadour were included. One was a capote, or blanket coat, fashioned in the Plateau style from a Hudson's Bay trade blanket and embellished with glass beads, and the other was a young girl's dress of red wool with beadwork adorning the shoulders, neckline and belt. The exhibit ran for a year. When it closed in 1988, the Lavadour dress was among two items purchased by the museum for the permanent collection.

Immediately following *Native Art to Wear,* the museum installed an exhibit that featured beaded clothing and accessories, *In Advance of the Drum: Great Plains Formal Dress.* The girl's dress by Lavadour was featured along with contemporary items of clothing. Included in the exhibit were contemporary photographs by Kenny Blackbird, Assiniboine, that featured people in formal clothing and conveyed the vibrant cultures of the Plains and Plateau regions.

In 1996, Lavadour was again asked to assist the museum. Staff member Gloria Lomahaftewa, Hopi/Choctaw, was working with beadwork scholars to research Plateau beaded bags in preparation for an exhibit that would feature the collection formed by gallery owner Elaine Horwitch. The Horwitch bags were not accompanied by cultural information or artist identifications, and the collector had recently passed away, making any informal information unavailable as well. Lavadour and other beadworkers and scholars traveled to the museum to review the approximately 400 Horwitch Collection bags as well as the museum's small group of Plateau beaded bags and cornhusk bags. Lavadour's comments and those of his colleagues were important additions to the content of the exhibit.

The exhibit, titled *Glass Tapestry: Plateau Beaded Bags from The Elaine Horwitch Collection,* was featured at the Heard for more than a year, then traveled to the Autry Museum of Western Heritage in Los Angeles and the Palm Springs Desert Museum in California. Lavadour and many other beadworkers had the opportunity to see the bags when they were displayed in the region of their origin at the Warm Springs Tribal Museum in Oregon.

Lavadour continued an informal association with the museum through the years through participation in the Heard Museum Guild Indian Fair & Market. His girl's beaded dress was featured in another exhibit in 1999 at the Heard Museum North. *Fashion Fusion* explored the ways in which Native fashion and mainstream fashion influence each other. In recent years, Lavadour was honored by the Tamastslikt Museum in Pendleton, Oregon, when he was asked to create a range of beaded and cultural object types that included horse trappings, men's and women's clothing, beaded accessories and a fully beaded cradleboard for the new museum.

Lavadour brings to the Masterworks series an extensive knowledge of technique as well as a skilled and creative sense of design. During the selection process he chose eighty objects from a field of several hundred beaded items from throughout North America. Among these are several miniatures, which Lavadour notes are a means for children to learn beadwork. As they grow older and more experienced, they apply their skills to full-scale objects.

Be Dazzled! includes some of the finest examples of beadwork and jewelry the museum has in its permanent collection. We are pleased that artists Maynard White Owl Lavadour, Gail Bird and Yazzie Johnson have given their time and knowledge to this project.

Diana F. Pardue is Curator of Collections at the Heard Museum.

BEADWORK

BY MAYNARD WHITE OWL LAVADOUR

I AM Maynard White Owl Lavadour, born and raised on the Confederated Tribes of the Umatilla Indian Reservation, which includes the Cayuse, Walla Walla and Umatilla people, near the city of Pendleton in northeastern Oregon. My ancestors were from the Cayuse, Palouse and Nez Perce tribes of the Eastern Plateau. Our tribal lands at one time included what is now southeastern Washington, northeastern Oregon and central Idaho. The stories and information that I will be sharing with you came from elders who were born and raised within these tribal territories.

I was asked to pick approximately eighty pieces of beadwork that I thought were of exceptional quality and beauty—masterworks—from the hundreds of beautiful examples in the Heard's permanent collection. I thought it would be a simple task until I began looking through all the cabinet drawers and shelves in the museum's vast storage area. In each cabinet I found pieces of such great craftsmanship that I thought they could not be surpassed. Yet for nearly four days I continued to uncover beaded treasures, each more magnificent than the one before. Perhaps "craftsmanship" does not do justice to the work. Each piece is artistry.

The majority of the beadwork was collected nearly a century ago. As a result, most of the pieces were made for personal use. Examining each piece, small or large, I learned much about individual tribes' beading and sewing techniques, designs, colors and materials. Above all, I learned about the importance that each artist placed on creating works of beauty and quality. In choosing the items for this book, I looked not only for physical beauty and quality of materials and construction, but also for the good feelings that can radiate from a piece.

My first thought was to group together items made with natural materials such as bone, animal claws, teeth, shells, feathers, hoofs, porcupine quills, ochre paints, rawhide, wood, seeds and animal pelts and hides. However, choosing beaded masterworks based solely on natural materials would not address distinct tribal characteristics or the evolution of beadwork over time. Most artifacts chosen were combined with trade goods such as glass beads of assorted colors and sizes, red, dark blue and green wool, and brass items such as bells, tacks and beads.

It is very important to realize that each tribe, or band, of Native people had its own unique traditional colors, designs, patterns, techniques and materials. Before the arrival of the Europeans, these aesthetic variables depended on each tribe's respective environment. After the introduction of trade goods, dramatic changes in the colors and designs of beaded cultural materials can be seen.

The quality of each finished piece and the materials used have always been very important in cultural arts. The beadwork tradition has been handed down in my family for nearly ten generations, with every generation learning from the elders. Many of my ancestors were master artists and their work was, and still is, highly sought after, both by family and non-Indian collectors. With each generation came change through the introduction of new materials and new ideas. The elders of each generation have seen this as a threat to our cultural heritage; as time passes we now can see that it has only strengthened it. Over the past ten generations, beadwork has become our way of life.

Mackenzie River moss bag (baby carrier), late 1800s

20 x 9. Velvet, glass beads, faceted steel beads, thread, canvas, leather. Gift of Florence D. Bartlett, Maie Bartlett Heard's sister, NA-NE-CR-Q-108.

Many colors are used in this cradle cover—pinks, yellows, ambers. It is an explosion of beauty. Beaded items allow infants to see beauty while still in their cradleboards.

People put their hearts and souls into cradleboards for the love of a new life going forward, and the child absorbs these good feelings of the maker as well as encouragement to grow up to be a master beadworker. Every Native group had its own style of baby carriers but each kept the infant snug, secure and safe. This Kiowa cradleboard is outstanding for the quality of its workmanship and for the amount of work it entailed. The maker chose ochre paints to complement the yellow beads. For Eastern Plateau people, the color gold, or yellow ochre, represents a golden land or heaven and has protective properties. Cradleboards protect our treasures. This one has miniature lanterns and thimbles on the sides. Many families blessed with master beadworkers who could afford beads gave their children two or three cradleboards that varied in size as the infants grew. Infants stayed in their cradleboards from birth to the age of six months or a year.

Comments accompanying objects are in the words of guest curator Maynard White Owl Lavadour.

Kiowa cradleboard, c. 1890

46 x 14 x 9.5. Glass beads, wood, buckskin, brass tacks, cloth, sinew, brass miniatures, thimbles. Fred Harvey Fine Arts Collection, 81BE.

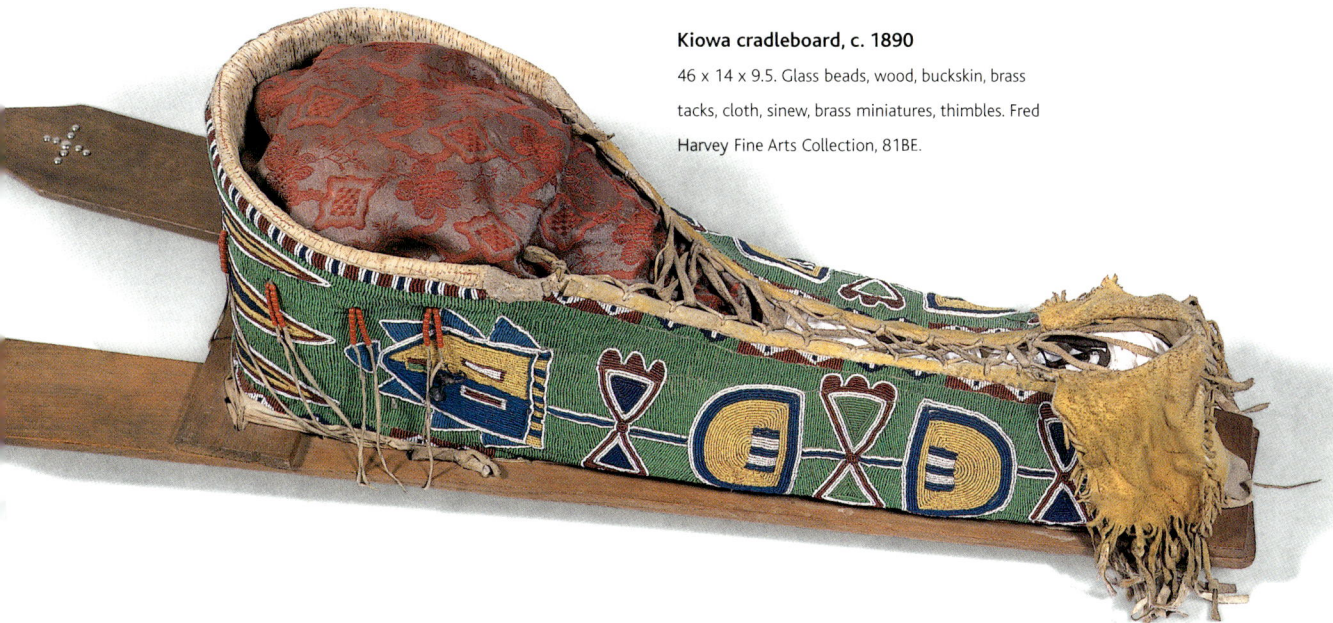

Plateau miniature cradleboard, early 1900s

9.25 x 3.5. Deer hide, glass beads, cloth, thread. Gift of Anne Burmister, NA-BS-SH-G-1.

It is possible to tell that this was made for a boy because of the wide beaded border.

To me, master bead artists are people who have been raised by and spent their whole lives working with their elders, learning all of the traditional skills, techniques, materials and stories relating to design, pattern and color. Along with the knowledge they have gained and their respect for their elders, these master beadworkers also possess a need to create masterpieces of great beauty, to honor our creator and their instructors. Growing up in a family of master artists that taught the traditional techniques on my reservation was a blessing for me. Now it is our turn as master bead artists to teach. The elders would tell us, "You share; teach whoever wants to learn. Make sure our family remembers."

Among most beadworking tribes, it was traditionally the women who did most of the beadwork. Among the Eastern Plateau tribes, it was common for beadwork to be created by both sexes, although the women continued to produce the majority of the work.

I was raised by my maternal grandmother, Eva Williams James Lavadour, for the first nine years of my life until her passing just before my tenth year. It was from my grandma Eva and her mother, Susie Williams, that I learned the traditional techniques of my tribes. My great-grandmother, Susie Williams, continued to teach me beading, cornhusk weaving, construction of clothing and horse outfits, hide tanning, parfleche painting, food gathering/storage and other traditional techniques needed to survive while living a traditional lifestyle. These master artists were born in 1902 and 1919, during a time when all these survival techniques were still needed and used by most tribal members from the Plateau. My great-grandmother Susie continued to teach and advise me until she passed on when I was twenty years old.

My great-grandma had a special little house to store family treasures she had inherited from her grandparents and great-grandparents. These items were from 100 to 200 years old, and they were her keepsakes, recalling those elders who taught and raised her. On many occasions while we were in the little house together, I would see her come across an old item and hold it close to her. These pieces would bring back fond memories of her childhood and her elders. The stories she told of our family and tribal history will stay with me the rest of my life. The elders would say, "Everything has a spirit, and we have to respect it, no matter what form it may come to us as. Just like us, they get lonely and need attention." This is why I have a great respect and love for artifacts in museum and private collections; I have been around similar pieces my whole life. Many of the items in my grandma's little house could have ended up in museum collections. A few did, but she chose to pass most of them on to us. Now it is our turn to respect these treasures and to give them the attention they need. They are now our keepsakes.

Beadwork is taught at a very early age. I began working with beads at age five and I started my children, eleven-year-old LeAnder and nine-year-old Suzette, at age two with stringing large beads. Stringing beads and threading needles was how I got my start. When my grandma thought I was ready to do actual beading, I started with miniatures so that I could learn the techniques and how to construct my project from start to finish in the shortest amount of time. It was our custom to give our first completed piece to a master bead artist to ensure our fast learning, nimble fingers and the quality of our future creations.

Instruction begins before children are even born. They are sung to and talked to, so that when it is time for them to come into this world, their births will come easy and fast.

When children are born, they are showered with many gifts made by the family to show their love, the greatest of which is a cradleboard that will be a secure home for at least the first year of life. Among the more prominent families, it was common for a child to receive two cradles because of the many skilled beadworkers in the family. Among my people, a cradle was made for each child and was not to be used for another.

Hupa necklace, c. 1850

32.75 x 2. Dentalium shells, glass beads, brass beads, thread. Fred Harvey Fine Arts Collection, 214BE.

The large cobalt blue beads were Russian trade beads.

When our elders taught us, they also encouraged us. They would always start each day with songs and prayers to our creator, and they would tell us to have a clean heart with good thoughts while working, no matter what we were working on. We were taught that our spiritual, emotional and mental state when creating or preparing items with your hands would affect whoever wore what we made or ate what we gathered and prepared. If these things were not done in the right manner, we were told, it could cause sickness.

Over the past twenty years, I have been very fortunate to have worked with many museum collections across the country, including the Heard's, and on many occasions I have felt a strong energy when holding certain items. I believe this to be a way of sharing the love that was present when the piece was being created. Even though the names of the artists and sometimes even their tribal origins are forgotten, the love in their hearts still exists in their work, as the love in our hearts when we are creating will always be strong, now and into the future, even after we have finished our work here on earth.

Today, many people believe that beadwork always has been a part of our cultural heritage, but colored glass beads were only introduced to my tribes on the Plateau within the past 200 years. Before the introduction of colored glass beads from Europe, we would decorate ourselves and our clothing with beautiful natural materials. Most of these materials were gathered within our own territories, but it was not uncommon for items to be traded from as far away as 1,000 miles or more. Trading networks and routes already were established and flourishing before European contact.

Before the use of beads, many kinds of shells—dentalium, cowrie, abalone and others—and feathers of the eagle, swan, woodpecker, flicker and other birds were used as ornamentation. Animal parts such as elk teeth, bone, horn, hoofs, hides of all kinds and hair from the porcupine and deer also were incorporated into decorative work. Porcupine quills were the natural material most used before the arrival of glass beads. The quills were cleaned, washed, dyed, sorted and then stitched down to create decorations for clothing and utilitarian items. Many quillworking techniques carried over to stitching glass beads into place.

Naturally produced colors—limited to ochre paints that came in red, indigo blue, green, yellow, orange, black and white—were used to brighten the decorative work. Light blue was used by my Cayuse and Palouse ancestors. Dyes from plants also were used, but dark colors were hard to produce. Of all the colors, blue was the most valuable because of its scarcity. This is why our painted rawhide containers were only outlined in blue. In pre-contact times, men's colors were blue, red and green, and women used all other colors. By the mid-1800s, all colors were used by both sexes because of the large quantities of beads that were available.

Distinctive designs, created by artfully blending colors and materials, identified beadwork by both tribe and time period. Early designs could be owned by tribes, individual families or individuals. Because of their use on utilitarian objects like rawhide containers and basketry, many of these early designs were very simple and most were geometric. My tribes and those east of the Rockies have many designs in common but, in most cases, the designs have their own meaning for each tribe.

The first beads introduced into my area came down the Northwest Coast with the Russians and with traders like the Hudson's Bay Company. These beads were quite large, with holes large enough to allow them to be strung on buckskin thongs, and they came in dark blue, light blue, forest green, amber and what we know now as chevrons. In the early 1800s, a smaller bead called a "pony bead" came into our possession. These beads came in white, black, white hearts, greasy blue, mustard and, in very small amounts, purple. By the late 1830s, an even smaller glass bead called a "seed bead" was introduced. Seed beads came in almost every color you could imagine.

Each tribe's location and distance from the Hudson's Bay Company's outposts determined when glass beads were first introduced to it and what colors and quantities were available.

Glass trade beads first arrived in small amounts, which is why early beadwork pieces have only the design outlined or filled in with beads on a colored wool or buckskin background. As larger quantities became available, design backgrounds began to be filled in using the contour method. We used this method because it is our belief that each contoured line of beads represented the spirit and life radiating from the main design, which in most cases was comprised of flowers, animals or people. It wasn't until the late 1800s that we began to fill in our backgrounds with straight rows of beads.

Among the Plateau people, large quantities of beads arrived just before our treaties were signed in 1855. Once we were put on reservations, more time was available because we were not allowed to travel long distances as we did in the past; we had to stay within our new boundaries. It was during the second half of the 1800s that our Plateau beadwork flourished. By the amounts of beadwork in this collection from the Plains and the Eastern Woodlands, we can see that this was true for all the beadworking tribes.

IN THE PAST, it was common for most of your family and tribe to produce beadwork but, today, many people can't find the time to work at their beading because of the many hours needed to produce individual pieces. Working with traditional materials is especially time consuming—a small item may take anywhere from a few days to a few weeks. Large items such as clothing and horse outfits may take months or sometimes years to complete.

I am very happy to include in the exhibit works by a number of contemporary bead artists. Each piece was made using traditional skills and techniques. A pair of fully beaded sneakers by Kiowa/Comanche artist Teri Greeves proves that we, as contemporary bead artists, are able to adapt with the times.

What a wonderful opportunity the Heard Museum has given me to once again work with its beadwork collection. In the past, I have seen only the Plateau beadwork. The beadwork collection is extensive and includes pieces from most of the beadworking tribes of North America. Working with this collection brought back many good memories and teachings from my elders, and I would like to thank the Heard Museum for giving me the opportunity to share this collection not only with my fellow bead artists, but also with the world.

I hope that the general public and collectors around the world will continue to admire, collect and preserve this very important art form. Many only see antique beadwork in museum settings, not realizing that there are many contemporary master bead artists making a living from their beadwork both off and on their reservations. Beadwork is thriving and in demand; there is no fear of its dying out.

To select eighty beaded masterworks was one of the most difficult, and most rewarding, challenges that I have faced as a bead artist. Working with the artifacts in the collection, I found it hard not to bond with the beadwork and the unknown artists who put their whole hearts and souls into creating these treasures of great beauty.

NORMA JAICHIMA
Huichol
Decorated gourd, 1982

13.5 x 10.5. Glass beads, gourd, beeswax. This beaded gourd received a first place award, a special award for beadwork and a special division award at the Heard Museum Guild Native American Arts Show in 1982. Gift of Mrs. James L. Coughlin, NA-MX-HU-I-42.

Norma Jaichima had a beautiful heart, and beadwork was how she expressed it. In the past, items such as this beaded gourd may have been associated with spirituality, a vision quest, healing or keeping the earth in balance. The gourd was covered with beeswax and the beads pressed into the wax. A particular effect is achieved by showing the central perforations of the beads rather than the rounded sides traditionally seen on beaded items.

Bags

Sioux teepee bag, late 1800s

28.5 x 26.5. Buffalo hide, glass beads, horsehair, tin cones, sinew, quills. Heard Museum Collection, NA-PL-SO-Q-53.

This bag is important because of its size, the detail of the design and the number of colors used. It is quite an accomplishment to keep the rows of beadwork straight on a bag this size. As a teepee bag, this was a container for personal items. It sat in the teepee and was seen from only the decorated side.

Sioux beaded handbag, c. 1900

9 x 13 x 4.5. Commercial leather purse, glass beads, faceted steel beads, sinew. Heard Museum purchase, NA-PL-SO-Q-69.

This is a nice example of combining contemporary elements with traditional techniques, materials, designs and colors. Items such as this show the outside influences that children experienced in school. Seeing things in books gave them ideas to explore and inspired them to make items that were not traditional.

Sioux bag, c. 1900

10 x 6 x 5. Deer hide, glass beads, thread. Heard Museum Collection, NA-PL-MIS-Q-21.

The maker of this bag—two of the three sides are shown here—was "going wild" with design and color. The bag is like a sampler, each side displaying a different design accomplished with differently colored beads. The shape is very non-traditional and three-dimensional. The shape and the drawstring make it more like a Victorian bag— which was possibly its inspiration—than a Native American bag from the time period.

Cheyenne tobacco bag, late 1800s

42.5 x 10 x 2. Deer hide, glass beads, goat hair, deer dew claws, sinew, brass bells, cornhusks, ochre. Fred Harvey Fine Arts Collection, 107BE.

This bag jumps at you with its striking design and use of color. Very small beads allowed for more detail in the design though they also meant nearly a week longer to do the work. A unique feature is the use of deer dew claws, which make a nice sound when the bag is in use. Other unusual features are cornhusks on the fringe, where quillwork would more typically appear, and the use of goat hair. The delicately detailed tassels have edge stitching, and the bag has fine fringe.

Cheyenne tobacco bag, late 1800s

36.5 x 9. Deer hide, cornhusks, flicker feathers, glass beads, sinew. Fred Harvey Fine Arts Collection, 108BE.

Some great features of this bag are the cornhusk wrapping and the small size of beads on the pouch. The flicker feathers on the side look dramatic next to the dark colors of the cornhusk wrap. They draw the eye, creating a balance with the tabs at the top. It is difficult to get cornhusks to hold color, especially green. Eastern Plateau people dry and grind lichen moss for green dye. They also use algae growing in ponds.

Cheyenne tobacco bag, 1890s

30 x 6. Deer hide, faceted glass beads, sinew, horsehair, tin cones. Estate of Carolann Smurthwaite, NA-PL-CH-Q-21.

The small size of the beads and the use of the yellow dyes make this a great bag. The bead-worker has to know in advance the number of hanks of beads that will be needed to complete an item so that they can be bought all at once. Later it is difficult to find the exact shades of color needed for matching.

Kiowa tobacco bag, late 1800s

31 x 5.5. Deer hide, faceted glass beads, paint, ochre, sinew. Fred Harvey Fine Arts Collection, 93BE.

Each tab and each side of this bag have their own designs and nicely chosen colors that draw the eye. The faceted, or cut, beads make the design glisten.

Kiowa tobacco bag, late 1800s

32.5 x 6. Deer hide, glass beads, thread. Fred Harvey Fine Arts Collection, 104BE.

The decorative tabs that fall from the top edge of this bag are a nice addition. The twisted fringe also adds to the overall effect. The shapes in the design are not traditional patterns. They seem to suggest churches.

Kiowa bag, late 1800s

18 x 3.5. Buckskin, glass beads, tin cones, brass beads, thread, mother of pearl. Fred Harvey Fine Arts Collection, 101BE.

This bag not only is beautiful, but also has a nice sound. The metal cones are all handmade from tin cans. Since they look clean, the writing may be on the inside. Once in a while, you come across a piece you just want to hold. I remember my grandma sitting and holding certain items, and that brought back all kinds of memories— how they were made, who made them. Though they were made in a time of great tragedy, still they were beautiful. I learned a lot about designs and what they meant from both of my grandmas. I asked a lot of questions, and my grandma would encourage me to remember by saying, "Put it in your heart and it will always be there."

Crow storage bag, late 1800s

26.5 x 13.5. Elk or buffalo hide, glass beads, sinew, thread.
Gift of Mrs. L.C. Wells, NA-PL-CR-Q-2.

This bag has simplicity, yet beauty.

Blackfeet or Crow container, 1939-1945

15 x 14 x 3.25. Deer hide, glass beads, sinew. Gift of
Mrs. Edward Manville, NA-PL-BL-I-1.

Normally a container of this shape was made of painted rawhide rather than beaded. This one has soft deer hide over finer rawhide. The larger red beads add character and stand out against the smaller beads in the background.

Plateau bag, late 1800s

7.5 x 5.8. Buckskin, faceted glass beads, brass beads, cloth, thread. Gift of Mr. and Mrs. Byron Harvey III, 3084-22.

The image looks as if it was taken from a Victorian card.

Iroquois bag, late 1800s

7 x 6. Glass beads, sequins, velvet, silk, cotton. Gift of Mr. and Mrs. Byron Harvey III, NA-NE-IR-Q-6.

Plateau, possibly Nez Perce, bag, late 1800s

10 x 9. Buckskin, glass beads, hemp, brass beads. Gift of Florence D. Bartlett, Maie Bartlett Heard's sister, 3280-68.

The design on this bag looks like it is vibrating; it's like the rippling effect one gets by throwing a rock in water. The maker used colors that were beautiful to him or her rather than actual plant or flower colors. This resulted in a more abstract design. The background contour adds more grace and life to the piece, and it took more time to accomplish than just beading straight across. Elders encouraged Eastern Plateau beadworkers to do contoured backgrounds. Another unique feature of this bag is that the beads are sewn with hemp rather than sinew. Around 1880, beadworkers used hemp to string beads and then cotton thread to sew down the strands.

Cree bag, early 1900s

6.5 x 6. Deer hide, ochre, glass beads, wool, thread. Gift of Mr. and Mrs. Byron Harvey III, NA-NE-CP-Q-24.

When early pieces like this one were made, there were not a lot of beads available so beadworkers would effectively contrast white beads with a dark background. This may once have been a legging—it slightly tapers at the top edge in the same manner as a legging. Eastern Plateau people sometimes formed bags from leggings when one of a pair was damaged or missing.

Plateau bag, early 1900s

12 x 9.38. Buckskin, glass beads, cloth, brass beads, thread. Gift of Mr. and Mrs. Edward Riley, NA-PL-MIS-Q-50A, B.

Sioux saddlebags, late 1800s

73 x 10.25. Buffalo hide, glass beads, sinew. Estate of Carolann Smurthwaite, NA-PL-SO-Q-63.

Cree bag, c. 1900

7 x 5.25. Wool, glass beads, buckskin, thread. Gift of Mrs. John C. Lincoln, NA-NE-PO-Q-2.

This is a beautiful container that would have been used on a horse. The long fringe looks nice when the horse is moving. With this sewing technique, only an accomplished and skilled beadworker can get the lines so straight.

The purple and red fringe adds a lot of character to this bag. The actual bag stops above the loom-beaded panel, while the loom beading at the bottom is part of the fringe. Indian people have creatively adapted the use of the different materials that were available at different times.

Crow bag, c. 1900

15 x 4.5. Buckskin, glass beads, brass beads, sinew.

Gift of Donald B. Cyrog, NA-PL-CR-Q-6.

The shape, the miscellaneous colored beads hanging from the fringe and the use of heavy brass discs on the fringe make this an outstanding bag. The maker painted the fringe and sides with ochre.

Kiowa paint pouch, c. 1900

12.25 x 3. Deer hide, mineral pigment, glass beads, sinew.

Fred Harvey Fine Arts Collection, 89BE.

Hard to obtain in large quantities, ochre paints were valued like gold and were traded from far distances among many different tribes. These small, cherished quantities were always placed in very special, highly decorated miniature paint pouches like this one. The bright reds came from the Plains.

Cheyenne tobacco bag, 1890s

30 x 6.5. Deer hide, glass beads, sinew, tin cones, wool. Estate of Carolann Smurthwaite, NA-PL-CH-Q-20.

The use of red wool brought out the design in the beadwork. There was a great variety of bead colors in the past. Although there are efforts to duplicate them today, it has not quite been successful.

Western Sioux tobacco bag, late 1800s

30.5 x 8. Deer hide, faceted glass beads, sinew, cowrie shells, steel beads. Heard Museum Collection, NA-PL-SO-Q-46.

All of the beautiful floral designs on the to of the bag are eye-catching. This bag is unique because of the large tabs at the base. The beadworker used colors you would not think were available at that time, such as the lime green.

Sioux tobacco bag, late 1800s

38 x 8.5. Buffalo hide, glass beads, quills, faceted brass beads, sinew. Fred Harvey Fine Arts Collection, 185BE.

The quality of the quillwork that embellishes this bag is exceptional, and the use of fringe adds a lot to the piece. The small beaded pocket at the top is unusual. It is hard to work with metal beads because their weight weakens the thread. The most successful use is with sinew, such as this beadworker used. It is interesting to note that the maker worked around a hole in the hide.

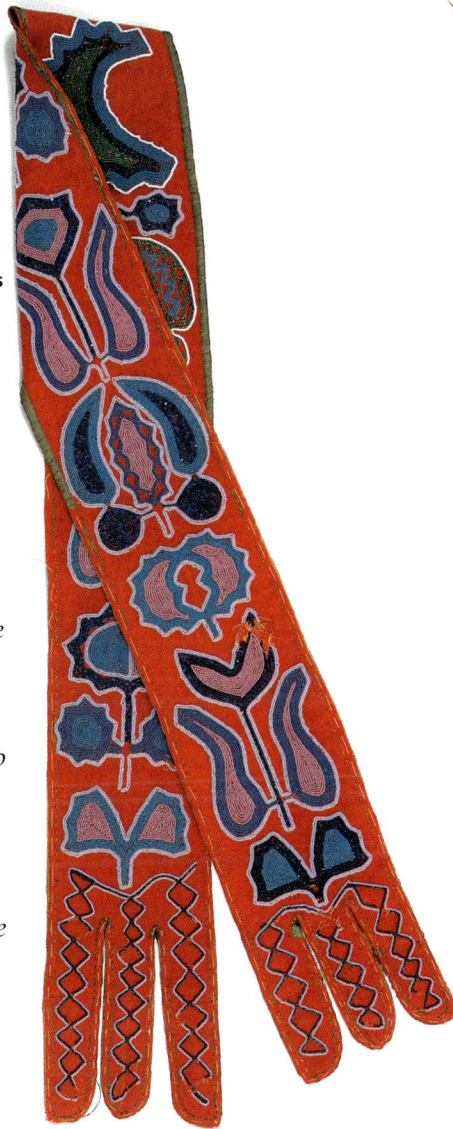

Creek bandolier strap, late 1800s

56 x 4.25. Felted wool, faceted glass beads, silk, thread. Gift of Louise Nevelson, NA-NE-IR-Q-10.

It takes a skilled and patient person to work with such tiny beads, but the result is a graceful design. Indian tribes all across the United States have a love of color and design that is expressed in pieces we make, such as this one. This strap has contour beading. The outlining was accomplished first, then the colors for leaves and flowers were chosen, and those areas were filled in with beads. This person put a lot of thought into the strap, balancing colors, shapes and designs.

Useful Objects

SADIE BOYD
Spokane
Saddle blanket, 1920-1930
34.5 x 54. Wool, glass beads. Gift of Mr. Greg Hofmann, NA-PT-SP-R-1.

The layout and choice of colors on this blanket are nice.

Otoe beaded blanket, 1940s-1950s
68 x 54. Wool, glass beads, thread, silk. Heard Museum Collection, NA-NE-CP-Q-23.

This is a well-balanced design. When this blanket was worn, the beadwork borders would hang down the front of the body of the wearer, making two parallel vertical shapes. Small beads were used, and they were sewn down every two beads. My grandma taught me to look at the reverse to see if there were any loops of thread or if the thread was stretched too far. You can tell by those features if the maker wanted to do the beadwork quickly or take time and do his or her best.

Blackfeet blanket strip, c. 1950

74.5 x 11. Buffalo hide, ermine, glass beads, brass beads, faceted steel beads, cloth, thread. Gift of Florence D. Bartlett, Maie Bartlett Heard's sister, NA-PL-BL-C-4.

Both the width and length of this blanket strip make it an impressive item. It is the largest I have ever seen, and it would have taken a long time to make since every four to five beads were sewn down. It would have been attached to a wearing blanket. When the wearer sat on a horse, the blanket strip would be placed on the lap, not only to protect the legs but also to show off the family's work. The ermine attached to this blanket was a sign of wealth.

Blackfeet knife sheath, 1939-1945

10 x 3. Buffalo or elk hide, glass beads, sinew. Gift of Mrs. Edward Manville, NA-PL-BL-Q-1.

It took a skilled person to sew beads onto hard leather like this buffalo or elk hide. Hide stretches and moves while it is being worked, making it difficult to keep the beads in balance. I have not seen many knife cases with qualities as good as this one has, especially in terms of the design, structure and function.

Crow horse collar, 1890s

36 x 18. Wool, glass beads, buckskin, brass bells, sinew. Heard Museum Collection, NA-PL-CR-Q-5.

Horse collars like this one really sound nice when the horse is in motion and you can hear the bells ringing. To hear a parade is as nice as looking at it. In one of the bells, the metal ringer has been replaced with two glass beads, making a different but pleasing sound. The red wool that shows from the background also looks nice. You would think it is beaded until you get close and realize it is the background.

Crow woman's stirrups, late 1800s

6 x 9.5 x 11. Moose or buffalo hide, wood, wool, brass tacks, glass beads, sinew. Gift of Mr. and Mrs. Byron Harvey III, NA-PL-CR-Q-8A, B.

Ojibwa bandolier bag, c. 1900

46 x 13.5. Wool, glass beads, cloth, thread. Gift of Dr. E. Robert Harned, NA-PL-MIS-Q-35.

There was a lot of time involved in this piece. In today's world, even with advantages such as electricity—not available to this beadworker—it would take three to four months of daily work to complete it. The yellow border edge is reminiscent of ribbon work, and it ties the separately beaded areas of the bag together. For many beadworkers, floral patterns represented the tree of life or healing herbs and foods that gave us life. My grandmas thought of this as part of our lives, not as art. If we didn't have elders, we would not have any of this. If we didn't have our children, we would not be carrying on these traditions.

Ojibwa bandolier bag, late 1800s

43.3 x 15. Wool, glass beads, cotton, yarn, mother of pearl. Acquired by the Fred Harvey Company from the Shoendorf Collection. Fred Harvey Fine Arts Collection, 118BE.

A lot of math is involved in beadwork. Try to picture the design and then visualize how to divide it into thirds. The beadworker must select a design that works in that space, but also goes with the other areas of the object. The beadworker chooses the designs and colors, and decides how to arrange it all. Sometimes designs were acquired through dreams or a vision quest, but generally the beadworker did not reveal the meaning.

Cheyenne miniature double saddlebag, c. 1900

7 x 2.75. Buckskin, glass beads, sinew. Fred Harvey Fine Arts Collection, 225BE.

Assiniboine gloves, c. 1900

9 x 6.5. Deer hide, faceted glass beads, sinew. Gift of Marion R. Plummer and Mr. and Mrs. Stanley Plummer, NA-NE-AS-G-2A, B.

These gloves have very nice beadwork; a good choice of colors and the inclusion of faceted beads works well. It took a skilled person to make such small and well-crafted gloves. Hide has a grain, just as cloth does. It needs to be cut from head to tail or it stretches and does not hang right. It is harder to make a miniature than a full-sized piece. It may be easier for children, because they are working more at their own scale. You learn at an early age, continue to bead all of your life, and your hands grow into your work. The quality improves over time. As you grow older and your eyesight diminishes, you go back to your earlier quality of work.

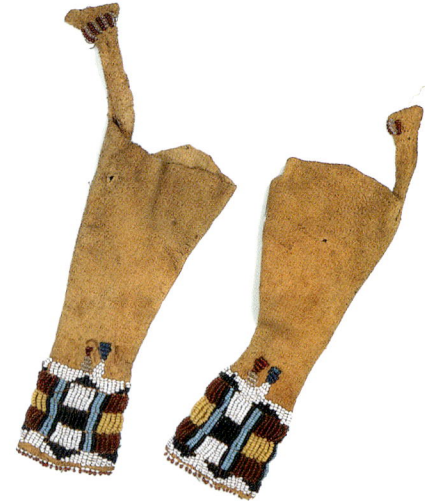

Southern Cheyenne miniature leggings, c. 1900

7.5 x 2.25. Buckskin, glass beads, sinew. Estate of Carolann Smurthwaite, NA-PL-SO-F-10A, B.

Often, children were involved with grandparents when making dolls. The children would help to make various aspects of the doll-sized leggings or belts. This would prepare them for making clothing. Children's clothes were exact miniatures of what adults wore.

Cheyenne miniature cradleboard, c. 1900

6.75 x 2 x 1.75. Glass beads, hide, wood, cotton cloth, sinew. Estate of Carolann Smurthwaite, NA-PL-SO-F-8.

Miniatures

Necklaces

Pomo necklace, c. 1900

18. Shell, cordage. Fred Harvey Fine Arts Collection, 96CI.

Kiowa necklace, late 1800s

25. Mescal beans, leather. Fred Harvey Fine Arts Collection, 76BE.

Blackfeet breastplate, 1939-1945

52 x 12. Buffalo bones, glass beads, brass beads, abalone shell, leather. Gift of Mrs. Edward Manville, NA-PL-BL-C-3.

The bones used in a piece like this breastplate were usually leg bones from buffalo or other large animals.

Plains necklace, late 1800s

16. Eagle or hawk talons, glass beads, brass beads, leather. Heard Museum Collection, 3205-50.

Hupa necklace, c. 1900

17.5. Dentalium shells, glass beads, thread, cloth. Fred Harvey Fine Arts Collection, 184BE.

The white dentalium shells in this 28-strand necklace are from the Northwest Coast.

Clothing

Kiowa shirt, 1870

35 x 47. Deer hide, ochre, glass beads, sinew. Fred Harvey Fine Arts Collection, 1BE.

This is simple, but dramatic. The periwinkle-colored beads vibrate against the green-colored fringe. The colors were used not only to paint the hide, but also to paint the fringe and small buckskin tassels on the front and back of the shirt. The shirt had beaded panels on the sleeves and on the shoulders at one time, but they were removed. Tufts of fringe also hang off the elbows. The tabs are the ankles of deer, and the hair was left on for decoration. It was common among Indian people to put beadwork over the seams; this provided one more opportunity to add beads to the piece.

Sioux moccasins, late 1800s

2.5 x 5 x 2.75. Deer hide, faceted glass beads, sinew, brass beads. Heard Museum purchase from Stanton Borum at Leupp Trading Post, Arizona, NA-PL-SO-C-14.

These are little jewels. Eastern Plateau chiefs traveled long distances to have counsel with other tribes. When they sat in a circle with their feet extended, the bottoms of their moccasins were visible. Beaded soles showed prestige.

Southern Arapaho woman's high top moccasins, late 1800s

25.5 x 10 x 3.5. Deer hide, buffalo hide, glass beads, sinew. Gift of Mr. and Mrs. Byron Harvey III, NA-PL-SO-C-50A, B.

The combination of yellow and red paint and the design of these moccasins is beautiful. Red balances the red outlining of the diamond pattern in the beadwork and makes it stand out. The overall construction is beautiful. Attaching a hard sole is difficult to do because it is sewn inside out, and then turned right side out after beading and before the rawhide dries completely.

Ute moccasins, c. 1900

24.5 x 10 x 3.5. Deer hide, glass beads, sinew, ochre. Heard Museum Collection, NA-SW-JA-C-3A, B.

These moccasins are unique. There is so much going on in the pattern with the zigzag and mountain designs.

Kiowa moccasins, late 1800s

20.25 x 6 x 3.25. Deer hide, buffalo hide, glass beads, sinew, pigment. Fred Harvey Fine Arts Collection, 23BE.

These are unique and the colors are very striking. They have braided fringe at the back of the heel and at the outside of the foot. When the wearer is on a horse, the fringe looks really nice.

Iroquois hat, late 1800s

11 x 5 x 4. Wool, glass beads, thread. Gift of Dr. E. Robert Harned,
NA-NE-IR-C-7.

*There are different bead sizes used in the
color shading of a single flower on this hat.
The blue zigzag bead trim at the bottom
brings out the blue in the flowers.*

**Southern Cheyenne or
Southern Arapaho girl's dress,
late 1800s**

32 x 30. Deer hide, glass beads,
cowrie shells, cotton cloth, sinew,
thread. Fred Harvey Fine Arts
Collection, 43BE.

*Natural materials and
trade goods combine in
this dress. The Native
tanned leather, ochre
paint and cowrie shells
from the Pacific Coast
make it very striking.*

Sioux vest, c. 1900

11.25 x 14. Glass beads, cloth, buffalo hide, sinew. Gift of Mr. and Mrs. Byron Harvey III, NA-PL-SO-C-59.

This is a unique way of decorating the edge with "white hearts," the red beads with white interiors. For a simple design, this really is bold and stands out.

Western Sioux boy's pants, late 1800s

11.75 x 13.75. Glass beads, buffalo hide, sinew, cloth, faceted steel beads. Heard Museum purchase, NA-PL-SO-C-99.

These boy's pants are rare. You usually only see these in photographs. They are fully beaded.

Blackfeet man's leggings, 1939-1945

30 x 13. Wool, glass beads, rayon ribbon, thread. Gift of Mrs. Edward Manville, NA-PL-BL-C-5.

It is unusual to see such a wide beaded legging strip. The red wool that borders the beadwork brings it to life.

Potawatomi vest, c. 1900

22.5 x 18. Wool, glass beads, mother of pearl and brass buttons, cotton thread, cloth. Gift of Mrs. John C. Lincoln, NA-NE-CP-C-33.

Both the front and back of this vest are unique and beautiful. The detail of the flower "veins" makes the design more prominent, and the geometric border at the bottom supports the design.

Sioux man's leggings, late 1800s

34 x 14. Deer hide, glass beads, sinew, brass beads. Fred Harvey Fine Arts Collection, 5BE.

Comanche man's leggings, late 1800s

42.5 x 19. Buckskin, ochre, glass beads, cotton cloth, thread. Fred Harvey Fine Arts Collection, 197BE.

The green-and-white candy stripe next to the fringe brings this piece to life. Usually just fringe is attached, but this has glass beads and brass beads and the decoration adds a lot to it. Each legging has a separate and unique attachment. The left leg has a single metal cone with red-dyed horsehair, while the right has a metal medallion with the words "Good Luck" written on it.

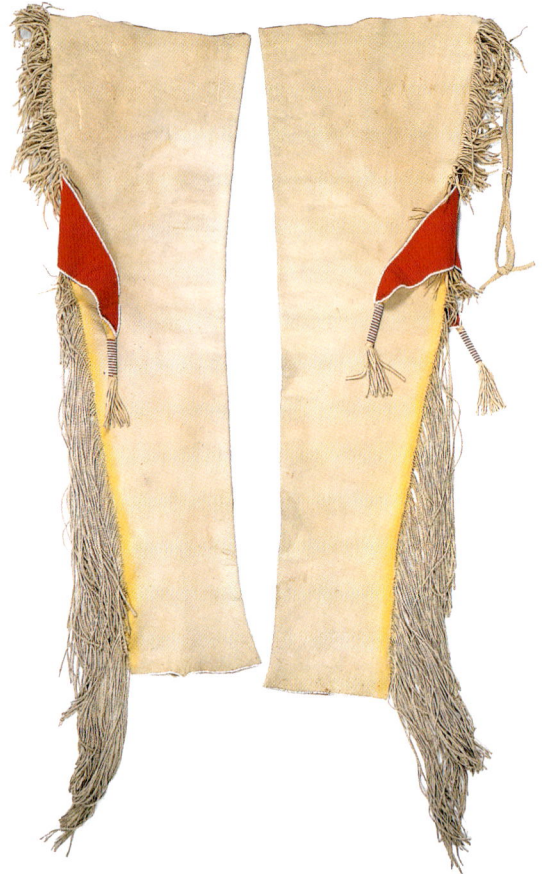

Even though this piece has minimal beadwork, it has some of the finest fringe I have ever seen. When the wearer rides a horse, the fringe hangs really nicely. Usually, the wearer will tie up the fringe when walking to avoid dragging it on the ground. The only way to get fine fringe is to use the underbelly of a deer. The bead trim at the ankles and the tassels with wrapped beadwork are also very nice.

JEWELRY

BY GAIL BIRD

FOR MOST PEOPLE, jewelry is basically an ornamental art. Among Native people of the Southwest, it can also be viewed as a functional art because it has been and can be used to define and identify peoples' places in their community. By wearing the proper ornaments at the proper times the wearer demonstrates awareness of his or her role in society. As an easy analogy, recall the time not so long ago when men wore suits and ties and women wore hats and gloves for a broad range of occasions. For Native people, jewelry served a similar purpose. People were not considered properly attired at ceremonies, either as participants or as observers, unless they were wearing their best silver or beads.

Comments accompanying objects are in the words of guest curators Gail Bird and Yazzie Johnson.

AS FORMAL CUSTOMS OF ATTIRE have given way for non-Indians, they have eroded similarly at tribal ceremonies and feast days. For participants, the proper jewelry is still considered essential. Among observers, it is usually only older Native people who dress for their roles, while the younger generations are as informally attired as their mainstream counterparts.

Early Native jewelry was made of shell, stone and turquoise. These simple materials formed the basis for the introduction and development of metal jewelry in the Southwest. Just as those early pieces were an integral part of Native life, as metalwork developed it too became part of the utilitarian and ceremonial component of that life. Thus, you see utilitarian objects invested with special care. Why else would anyone spend so much time hand-filing ridges and planes onto a simple silver button? Why create dozens of matching buttons for the strap of a pouch, or an ornament for a leather bowguard, unless the object itself had a singular importance to Native people?

While function was not the only reason for the flowering of metalwork in the Southwest, it definitely provided cause for a silversmith to stretch his skills and imagination, and to find satisfaction and pride

RODERICK TENORIO
Santo Domingo, b. 1955
Bolo tie, 1994

23.75 x 3. Number 8 turquoise,
silver, leather. Purchased by the
donors at the Heard Museum
Guild Indian Fair & Market.
Gift of Richard and Lois Rogers,
4028-1.

in producing a special object or executing a difficult technical feat. This becomes especially evident in the work of the 1940s and 1950s, when individual artists' names begin to emerge. This marks a transition, a time when the craft of jewelry making began to be recognized as an art and jewelers began to cater to a new and different consumer—the non-Indian collector.

Most of the Heard's vast jewelry holdings predate 1970, anchored by the magnificent Fred Harvey Company and C.G. Wallace collections. It also includes fine examples of early Navajo silverwork, a few pre-Columbian gold pieces, a few German silver Plains items, Anasazi shell and turquoise. The contemporary collection is built around the early and classic works of Charles Loloma, who more than any other artist changed the look of Indian jewelry and ideas about its nature. There is also a small but growing collection of work by living jewelers who are pushing the boundaries that define Indian jewelry.

With thousands of such pieces in the collection, the task of selecting great work was a daunting one. Where does one begin? How does one define a masterwork? How do you pick work that will dazzle?

According to *Webster's Dictionary,* a masterwork or masterpiece is "a thing done with masterly skill or

as a great work of art or craftsmanship." Everyone has an idea of what that means. Great beauty, flawless technique and quality of materials are obvious parts of the whole. In handcrafted work, there is also the mark of the individual, the burst of creative spirit that guides skilled eyes and hands.

This selection includes choices that many will see as obvious—important works that have been featured in numerous Heard Museum exhibitions and publications. Other choices may cause some to question our judgment or knowledge.

Yazzie and I are both self-taught. Our education has included reading about, looking at and studying traditional Southwest arts. Looking at the complex subtleties of design in jewelry, pottery, textiles and baskets has made us aware of the skill that is involved in understated simplicity and that has guided our personal work. Yazzie's first attempts at metalworking closely follow the historical development of early Navajo work. By understanding the time and place in which a work was originally produced and knowing which primitive tools were used to construct an item, we have been given a greater appreciation for completed objects. In noting the meticulous attention given to details of finishing, we recognize the importance of individual excellence, ideas and skill.

LEO POBLANO
Zuni, 1905-1959
Box, 1950s
3.34 x 3.74. Silver, spondylous shell, turquoise, jet, shell. Fred Harvey
Fine Art Collection, 348S.

This is a collaborative piece made for the tourist trade, probably at the instigation of C.G. Wallace. The inlaid lid is Zuni, but the box is Navajo-made, highly stamped with the lines and ridges that appear in row bracelets, although with a much smoother texture. The feet were made by making buttons and then joining them together to form beads. Decorative designs appear on both sides of the button-shaped feet. The hinge was made by forming pieces of silver into coils, connecting them and then adding a very elaborate piece of stamp work. It is similar to a rivet on a large door. There is also elaborate stamp work and a great scalloped-edge bezel that holds the shell on top. The interior is perfectly crafted. This box was made for the tourist trade, not Native use. It is a great example, a rare example, of a time when the collaborative process met consumer demand to create really fine pieces of art.

That recognition of the importance of the individual guided our selections. We have chosen works by individuals whose creative genius is expressed in pieces that demonstrate complex thought and absolute skill, and we have also chosen some works of complex thought not matched by craftsmanship but instead by patience. There are also pieces here that are small in scale and made of relatively inexpensive materials, some pieces stark in their simplicity and others so finely embellished that they made us yearn for the time when people had—or took—the time to achieve such perfection. We found these items to have merit and importance equal to that of the larger, more valuable pieces. While many such examples are included here, five of them seemed especially notable to us.

AN EXAMPLE OF SHEER ELEGANCE, complexity and skill is the early plain silver bridle. When you look carefully and begin to dissect the piece—forgetting that it is an ornamental trapping for a horse—you can see pins, buttons and earrings as well as bracelet and concho belt parts. In one magnificent piece, you have many small components perfectly and simply crafted, linked together with silverwork of understated severity. It seems simple only until you know that the silverwork was hand-forged and that the smooth surfaces required hours of heating, hammering, hand-filing and sanding. We had the privilege of being able to handle and feel how the flat surfaces were formed and to see the many underlying facets that marked the hammer blows. The silversmith's final assembly perfectly balanced the many intricate details and created an object of grace and proportion.

ONE OF OUR FAVORITE PIECES, and one we thought about quite a bit, is the single bag (page 44) we have included. The collection had many outstanding examples, but as we looked closer and examined this particular one carefully, the intricacy of its design far outweighed its shortcomings in craftsmanship. We decided that the piece was not the work of an individual artist, but an assembled piece based on one individual's carefully planned and constructed idea and design. The buttons on the strap

Navajo bridle, c. 1900

6 x 20.5 x 11. Silver, leather. Fred Harvey Fine Arts
Collection, 424S.

*Bridles are composed of many parts.
If you took this apart you would have
pins, buttons and concho belt parts—
jewelry for people. By linking them
together, you move that idea over to
the idea of dressing a horse. This piece
is perfectly balanced in its simplicity.
The large, spectacular conchos are
joined by smooth, flat surfaces. Long
surfaces allow your eyes to rest
between elements.*

Navajo bag, c. 1900

34 x 6.5. Silver, leather, glass beads, turquoise. Fred Harvey Fine Arts Collection, 422S.

The buttons on this piece were made by different people. The oldest ones are probably those on the shoulder straps, and they become more elaborate as they go down. Each two or four are by a different maker. The maker waited the time it took to gather all the materials, and thought of how to balance them after all of the years of collecting and planning. In a way, that is the way a lot of people work now. You do not have everything all at once, but you have an idea, and you develop toward it.

are simple, very plain, but at the ends of the strap joining the bag are large buttons made from liberty head quarters, and here the ideas begin to flow.

The decorative buttons on the sides of the front do not all match, but they are horizontally matched pairs. The larger buttons all have a similar scalloped edge. The single heart-shaped button is probably not Southwestern, but maybe Mexican or Plains. The center of the bag is dominated by a large appliquéd piece of floral beadwork. When you look at the piece, you can see the connection between the scalloped edges of the buttons and the curvilinear lines of the beadwork flowers.

When we lifted the flap of the bag, we found that the interior was made of leather heavily stamped with flowers—probably recycled leather from a Mexican tooled bag or scabbard. The sheer complexity of the piece and the repetition of the floral motif from the interior unseen part of the bag to the visible exterior front were delightful to see. In terms of conception, the notion of gathering, waiting and assembling like items to complete a work is not new. To see it pulled together so successfully in an early piece was a wonderful surprise.

THERE ARE TWO PIECES that we chose that fit the "small in scale and relatively inexpensive" category. The first is a very simple lined button made from a coin. What is notable about this piece is the way in which the lines were put on the surface. First, the button was gently domed from the underside, then each line was hand-filed at an angle. When the button is viewed from the side, you get a sense of dimension as you note the depth of scale between each file mark. That volume creates a sense of monumental form in this small object.

Navajo button, 1920s

1.62 x .5. Silver. Fred Harvey Fine Arts Collection, 42S.

THAT SENSE OF MONUMENTALITY also exists in a piece that is barely an inch-and-a-half high. It is a Zuni carving in turquoise by Leekya Deyuse of a man carrying a large water canteen on his back. The figure is bowed with the weight of his burden. The face has gritted teeth and a look of intensity and concentration. Corded sinew interacts with the carving at the strategic points of the handles of the canteen, cradling the vessel and supporting the weight across the figure's back. The addition of the cord accentuates the heaviness and adds dimension to the strained posture.

The figurative carvings and inlaid jewelry from Zuni are well known for their artistry; among the best examples are the depictions of human figures. What we found striking were the somber, almost sad expressions on all the faces. Whether they were Indian or Anglo, like our small turquoise man or the famous Harvey girl figure by Leo Poblano, all the faces wear similar pensive expressions. These pieces possess such humanity that they prompt a response that includes both smiles of admiration and deeper feelings of recognition, warmth and empathy.

ATTRIBUTED TO LEO POBLANO
Zuni, 1905-1959
Inlaid figure, 1939
5.75. Shell, silver, jet. Gift of Mr. and Mrs. Byron Harvey III, NA-SW-ZU-J-334.

The front of this piece has character and whimsy, along with wonderful imagery. The back is almost as exciting because you do not have to decorate the functional part of the piece, but when you do it indicates how important it is. The intricate stamp work that went into this is almost as exciting to a jeweler as the front inlay piece. This is so detailed that the figure actually has eyelashes and eyebrows, and the surface of the pie is bubbling.

LEEKYA DEYUSE
Zuni, 1889-1966
Carved figure, 1927
1.5 x 1 x 1.25. Turquoise, sinew. Gift of C.G. Wallace, NA-SW-ZU-F-49.

FRANK DISHTA
Zuni, 1902-1954
Earrings, 1936

1.5 x 8. Silver, turquoise. Gift of C.G. Wallace, NA-SW-ZU-J-246.

ANOTHER small but beautiful item is a pair of inlaid Zuni earrings of silver and turquoise (above). They measure about one-and-a-quarter inches by three-quarters of an inch. Everything is impressive about this pair—the color and quality of the turquoise, the composition between the four center diamonds and the surrounding pear shapes, and the added bonus of seeing the spaces between the points of the pears and diamonds set with small, irregular cuts of stone. Between each scallop on the exterior edge are tiny silver balls that add dimension to the surface. There is a gentle curve to each earring, and each stone has the look of being individually cut and finished. Like so many Zuni pieces from the Wallace Collection, these earrings illustrate time, patience and attention to detail.

UNLIKE THE ARTS OF POTTERY, weaving and basketry, which have long histories of use and development in the Southwest, jewelry in metalworking form is relatively new. Prehistoric jewelry of the Southwest was originally crafted from stone, shell, bone and wood using tools made from basically the same materials. The qualities of skill, precision and selection of materials is evident in many surviving pieces, such as a strand of turquoise beads from the Anasazi period. This style of work continues today most notably in Santo Domingo Pueblo, where work of equal brilliance incorporates changing designs and new materials, such as the shaded ten-strand olivella shell necklace by the late Charles Lovato (both pieces shown on facing page).

Other materials and styles characteristic of early jewelry can still be seen today, even though hand-crafting techniques have been augmented with metal drills and electric-powered grinders. The work continues because of its importance to the people. The scarcity of natural turquoise makes pieces such as Jose Reano's 1980s-era turquoise necklace (facing page) increasingly rare. His regard for the material is reflected in his respectful handling of it. By not grinding away too much of the valuable stone and by not removing all traces of matrix, as once might have been done, he achieves a look reminiscent of older handcrafted pieces.

Metal and metalworking techniques were introduced to the Navajo in the mid-1800s. Because of the near-simultaneous introduction of tools, techniques and materials, in the beginning Southwest silverwork showed a notable consistency of style. As technology and ideas spread, various styles began to emerge, usually associated with tribal affiliation.

Early styles are widely recognized as Navajo by the massive use of silver and the selective use of turquoise; Zuni by the lighter use of silver and multi-stone design complexity; and Hopi by graphic silver overlay. Within those broad categories are clear delineations of individual style and technique. For example, the massive bold look of heavy Navajo silver can be achieved by using thick metal and cutting or filing away the surface, or by pounding and forming the metal from behind to create the look of solid, heavy silver. Eventually, stark simplicity gives way to bold surface decoration, but there is still something about the work that gives it the unmistakable look and feel of Navajo.

In all areas, work changes slowly over time. The innovations that take place are partially determined by the changing market and the non-Native consumer with different requirements. Silver and

Ancestral Pueblo necklace, 900-1115 AD
20. Turquoise, spondylous shell. Fred Harvey Fine Arts Collection, 202BE.

This elegant necklace of very fine turquoise beads was made before Europeans came into the Southwest. What is remarkable about this piece is the quality that was achieved using crude stone tools.

CHARLES LOVATO
Santo Domingo
Necklace, 1970-1980
12. Olivella shell, white shell, tortoise shell. Gift of Mr. and Mrs. Alfred Tomlinson, 4032-1.

Innovative jeweler Charles Lovato was one of the first people in Santo Domingo to blend colors in rolled bead necklaces. He introduced the use of a lot of color and diverse materials to Santo Domingo jewelry. This simple and elegant ten-strand necklace is made of shell that has been rolled very fine.

JOSE REANO
Santo Domingo
Necklace, c. 1970
22.25. Lone Mountain turquoise, spondylous shell, coral. Acquired by the donor from Don Hoel, Sedona, Arizona around 1971. Gift of Mareen Allen Nichols, 4033-31.

The natural turquoise in this necklace has little wear, so it is still uniform in color and lacks the polish that develops through use. With time and wear, the turquoise would have changed from solid blues to a mix of blue and green. Reano was not trying to get the turquoise all exactly smooth, as there are areas where the matrix comes out. He chose not to grind away too much of this scarce material, knowing that in the old pieces that was how it was handled. He is not looking for perfection but for an expression of the old ways that respects the material.

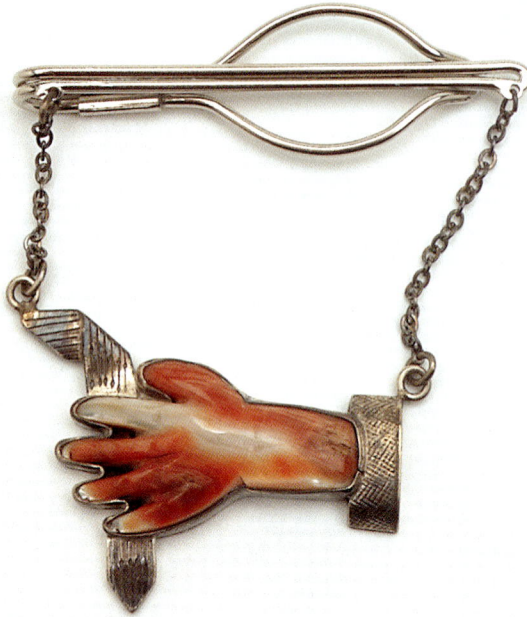

LEEKYA DEYUSE
Zuni, 1889-1966
Tie bar, 1930s-1950s
2.5 X 2. Silver, spondylous shell. Gift of C.G. Wallace,
NA-SW-ZU-J-193.

This tie bar is a wonderful little statement about one culture making something for another culture. Or, it could be just a humorous statement about wearing a suit and tie.

turquoise are still the dominant materials, although individual pieces have become smaller and lighter in weight. New products such as tie bars, bolo ties and boxes are made. While some pieces are quickly and cheaply produced to fill the growing demand, superb and highly individual work is also crafted, such as the wonderful Leekya Deyuse tie bar with the spondylous shell hands and silver tie (above). The influence of traders makes the Navajo and Zuni collaborations from the C.G. Wallace Collection possible. The great silver and inlaid boxes and figures are prime examples of this.

T H E 1 9 5 0 s mark the beginning of the period in which work is associated with named individuals. This is the inception of the modern period, and no two jewelers have influenced it more than Charles Loloma and Kenneth Begay.

The early, bold, simple tufa cast designs of Loloma and his experimentation with technique and finished look is comparable with the evolution of the minimal stamp work and elegant hammered forms of Begay. Both artists began with traditional techniques, then stretched those methods to create new

and distinctive looks. Loloma's dramatic experiments with color, materials and texture helped lead the way, as did Begay's streamlining of basic design forms, toward what people have grown to accept as Indian jewelry.

The sheer volume and scope of the Heard Museum's collection of work from 1890 to 1970 dictated that the majority of our selections would come from that period, but the inclusion of modern pieces is not an afterthought. The work of the last thirty years varies from excellent traditional work produced in recognition and emulation of a particular cultural style to works involving contemporary metalworking techniques, materials and ideas. The availability of travel, education and training and the ability to be receptive to both old and new ideas mark the work of the best of the new generation of artists.

There is continuity of excellence in terms of skill and craftsmanship; technological advances would not permit otherwise. But there is more than technique present. As with all great art, it is the individual personality and interests of the artist that determine his or her direction and interpretation of the medium.

Artists whose works are as visually diverse as Cheyenne Harris and Perry Shorty illustrate this point. Both are equally involved in the process and technical aspects of metalworking. Where Harris experiments with relatively new techniques such as surface texturing and combining metals to create designs, Shorty re-creates older, little-used processes including hand-forging metal and hand-pulling wire. Both create works of stunning simplicity and distinctive ornamentation. Both pay attention to the most minute details such as embellishing the underside of an object or individually crafting the many small graduated silver balls that delineate a point or an edge. Both carry on in the tradition of the best jewelers in the collection. Their works possess the unmistakable look and feel of Navajo jewelry.

That unmistakable look and feel is part of what defines a masterwork. Whether Indian jewelry is created for a Native or non-Native audience, the pleasure one gains from owning or wearing a fine example extends to include the artist who created it and the viewer who admires it. It is part of the evolving cycle of being a participant and observer in the long history of jewelry in the Southwest. It is our hope that readers will come away from this project with admiration and respect for work created by artists for the enjoyment of others. Working with the collection has been a source of renewal of both those qualities, and a renewal of inspiration, for the two of us.

KENNETH BEGAY
Navajo, 1913-1977
Purse button, c. 1960

2.5. Silver, ironwood. Estate of Carolann Smurthwaite, NA-SW-NA-J-715.

Formed of ironwood with a very simple cut-out piece of silver over it, this pin has the clean, modern, contemporary look characteristic of so much of Kenneth Begay's work. The design echoes the simple water-like shapes that people now think of as representing rivers. As early as the 1950s, Begay was doing things that were not very Indian-looking, and yet he still had strong stylistic and technical ties to the past. Even today, his work would be defined as not very Indian-looking.

Shell inlay

JUAN DE DIOS
Zuni, 1882-1940s
Bowguard, 1920

4.5 x 3.25 x 1.6. Silver, spondylous shell, turquoise, leather. Gift of C.G. Wallace, NA-SW-ZU-J-292.

This bowguard has boldness, a contrast of colors and an openness, plus symmetrical flow. It also has really fine stamp work along the edges.

JOHN GORDON LEAK
Zuni
Pin, 1940s

3.63 x 3. Silver, turquoise, coral, jet. Gift of C.G. Wallace, NA-SW-ZU-J-184.

This is an incredible example of work. Technically, it is perfection. The scallops on the edges echo the design and add volume. Alone, the black would have been starkly simple, but those little scallops on the edge lighten it and make the butterfly float. They give it light, give it air. And all the turquoise set individually around the edges matches in color. While we're not sure if John Gordon Leak or another artist did the silverwork, the person who did this had the confidence that he could solder the whole thing in three phases. First, he had to solder down the bezels. Next, he put in the wiring that is between the round balls and the centerpiece. Last, he added on the little balls while it was still a flat sheet. The heat used to solder all the small pieces onto the flat sheet could have caused the piece to collapse or caused the little balls to move, destroying the design.

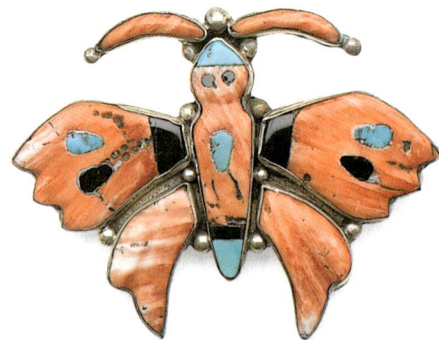

LEEKYA DEYUSE
Zuni, 1889-1966
Inlaid shell, 1928

2.13 x 2.75. Spondylous shell, turquoise, jet, silver. Gift of C.G. Wallace, NA-SW-ZU-J-322.

Zuni shell, early 1900s

3.6 x 3.5 x 1.2. Spondylous shell, turquoise, jet. Fred Harvey Fine Arts
Collection, 1399CI.

*This is a beautifully crafted piece with turquoise all
from the same period. The color matches from
stone to stone, and it is obvious that the stones are
natural, with changes in coloration occurring
naturally. This gives the piece an added dimension.
The shell is very thick, and the amount of turquoise
that goes into this piece is impressive. Turquoise is a
by-product of silver, gold and copper. Since it is not
productive for the mining industry to mine the
same way they did in the past, the quality of
turquoise today is not good; it has often been
stabilized or dyed. The old pieces were made with
great material and cannot be duplicated today
because the material is just not there. The richness
of the color in the old turquoise is really beautiful.*

LEEKYA DEYUSE
Zuni, 1889-1966
Inlaid shell, 1930s-1950s

1 x 3.2. Spondylous shell, turquoise, jet, shell. Gift of C.G. Wallace,
NA-SW-ZU-J-66.

*Leekya Deyuse carved underneath the
butterfly's body of spondylous shell, inlaid the
turquoise on top of it and then smoothed it
down so that there is one smooth surface. The
scalloped edge has great detail, giving the
impression that the butterfly is floating. Earlier
pieces such as this one were so graphic. They
were so simple. They were meant to be seen
from a distance. In a culture where people do
not stand as close to each other as in some other
cultures, these were made to be seen from four
or five feet away or across the plaza. This is
where their actual impact is—from a distance.*

Useful elegance

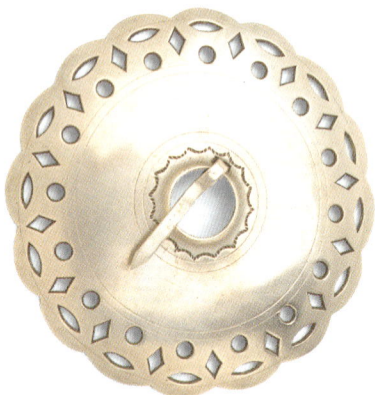

Caddo brooch, early 1900s

2. German silver. Heard Museum purchase, NA-PL-MS-J-2.

The German silver brooches are among the simplest pieces in the collection. Compared to the heavy Navajo pieces, there is a lightness and a delicacy about them. The pierce work adds to this.

Navajo concho, early 1900s

3.75 x .75. Silver. Fred Harvey Fine Arts Collection, 161S.

The really bold repoussé in the center of the floral leaf design, combined with the leaf-like stamp work on the corners, gives this piece directness and balance. Also, the scalloped edge makes it impressive.

CHARLES BITSUIE
Navajo
Button, 1933

1.62 x .5. Silver. Gift of C.G. Wallace, NA-SW-NA-J-267.

Zuni pin, 1930s-1940s

2.5. Silver, turquoise, coral, jet, shell. Gift of C.G. Wallace, NA-SW-ZU-J-306.

This pin has extremely complicated lapidary work and attention to detail, along with a nice, simple bezel with stamp work along the edge. We chose smaller things intentionally, because when you are looking at detail, you are looking at the intricacy of work. If you look at a small object, the complexity of it is magnified because of its very size.

Navajo comb, 1920-1930

2.75 x 2.3. Silver. Fred Harvey Fine Arts Collection, 1176S.

This comb is technically amazing. It is a combination of repoussé work, stamp work and incredible saw work to make the teeth. The metal between the teeth was filed and then sandpapered so that each of the tines is smooth.

Navajo powder horns, 1956

5.9. Silver. Fred Harvey Fine Arts Collection, 535S.

These were chosen for their weight and design … and to answer the question of a younger generation, "What are those?"

Navajo canteen, 1920-1940

4 x 3 x 1.25. Silver. Fred Harvey Fine Arts Collection, 594S.

This is a double-sided canteen with appliquéd tufa cast designs.

EDISON CUMMINGS
Navajo, b. 1962
Teapot, 1996
6.625 x 12.25 x 6.5. Silver, ironwood. Heard Museum purchase from the Heard Museum Shop, 3637-1.

This teapot is extremely well crafte and has a modern look. The angle or turn of the handle contrasts ver well with the elegant upturn on th spout. There is a pointed guard on the handle, providing a place for t lid to rest gracefully. The teapot is reflective of Kenneth Begay's work—the simplicity of lines, the straight, heavy, solid stamp work and the use of ironwood. Cummings and Begay both worke at the White Hogan in Scottsdale, Arizona, though at different times. but Cummings' work takes on a special quality of its own—his forms and shapes depart from tho of other silversmiths.

CHEYENNE HARRIS
Navajo/Northern Cheyenne, b. 1963
Flatware, 1997
9.875 x 1.25. Silver, white and yellow gold. Heard Museum purchase from the Heard Museum Shop, 3638-1.

Cheyenne Harris has combined her training in contemporary metalsmithing with her own ideas of design. The set is highly stylized, with an abstract look and feel. The sides and the backs are just as interesting as the fronts. We see many of the tiny little touches so important in early Navajo work, added not just for function or stability, but for sheer beauty and exuberance. On Harris's fork, a line of gold has been added to the back of the tine, introducing a very subtle change in color, marked by a geometric inclusion. When you turn the fork over, you see the same line on the top of the center tine, only more pronounced. The contrast between the matte finish and shiny surfaces is reminiscent of early Navajo stamp and file work. But here, instead of it being a contrast between light and dark, there is a change in texture.

LEEKYA DEYUSE AND DAN SIMPLICIO
Zuni, 1889-1966 and 1917-1969
Bowguard, 1948

5 x 3.5. Turquoise, coral, silver, leather. Dan Simplicio Jr. identified the carved coral as the work of his father. Gift of C.G. Wallace, NA-SW-ZU-J-291.

The carved bears and the polished natural chunks of branch coral form a pleasing contrast. The piece also has wonderful stamp elements appliquéd onto the surface of the base. The central figure has a big, bold piece of twisted wire around it, adding volume and making the piece multidimensional. When it was first worn, the silver was very shiny. The black leather would have shown through the pierce work and would have outlined and made the central figures appear to be floating in space. The attention to detail and the massive use of materials make this a very important piece.

Navajo bowguard, early 1900s

2.25 x 2.5 x 3.6. Silver, leather, turquoise. Gift of Mrs. Samuel G. Shannon, NA-SW-NA-J-389.

The piercing of the stone indicates that this piece of turquoise came from a necklace. The heart-shaped cast elements are nice. A row of tiny little buttons defines one edge, a step toward pure decoration, but added only on one side. On the other side, the leather is pierced, which gives similar emphasis in terms of detail, but in leather rather than metal. It is a nice attempt at achieving balance and symmetry.

Navajo bowguard, c. 1900

2.75 x 2.6 x 2.75. Silver, leather, turquoise. Fred Harvey Fine Arts Collection, 164S.

This is not miniature jewelry, but it is jewelry that is made for a child. It shows the importance of jewelry to the people. It was made to scale—the stamps are smaller, the stone is smaller—to fit a child's wrist.

Bracelets

TOM KEE
Navajo
Bracelets, 1956
2 x 2.38 x .75. Silver, turquoise. Fred Harvey Fine Arts Collection, 526S and 519S.

These two bracelets have a nice, heavy, bold look to them, but the wonderful parts are the bracelet ends —hands have been carved and sleeves, rows of buttons and bracelets are detailed. The bracelet itself is like a pair of arms—you can see the musculature, and the arms are bent as if caressing. The stamps are great and accent the shape.

Navajo bracelet, c. 1900
1.8 x 1 x 2.8. Silver. Gift of the Graham Foundation for Advanced Studies in the Fine Arts, NA-SW-NA-J-549.

The deer's head was carved from a tufa cast ingot. It was then stamped and appliquéd to the center of the bracelet in the same way that a stone would be set in a bezel.

Navajo bracelet, c. 1920

2.8 x 1 x 1.8. Silver, turquoise. Gift of Woodards' Indian Arts,
NA-SW-NA-J-173.

The stone and bezel were recessed into the stamped metal, creating a smooth surface.

Navajo bracelet, 1890-1900

2.3 x 1.78 x 1. Silver. Fred Harvey
Fine Arts Collection, 1072S.

This is a great example of a forged bracelet with simple file and repoussé work. The three repoussé sections are balanced and symmetrical, filling the space yet leaving a lot of negative space that allows the eye to rest. The silversmith has taken a file to smooth away the surface to create surface texture.

This is coin silver. You can see little cracks in the metal that occurred when the artist pounded and bent the bracelet. You get telltale cracks, showing what the metal went through.

Navajo bracelet, 1900-1920

1.5 x 2.4 x .75. Silver. Fred Harvey Fine Arts Collection, 73S.

Four stamps used over and over created this design.

Navajo bracelet, 1970s

2.25 x 2.5 x 3. Bisbee turquoise, silver. Gift of Mr. and Mrs. Henry Galbraith, 3309-32B.

In this bracelet, the focus is on the stones. This Bisbee turquoise is probably the rarest, with the deep dark blue and the deep chocolate brown matrix. The stones are very hard and will always retain their colors. If a silversmith gets the chance to work with stones like these, the smith will do his or her best work because the turquoise is so rare. In this bracelet, the surrounding elements echo the stones, so you focus on the stones and move your eyesight into these other elements. All the silver elements around the double stones echo the simple setting, drawing your eyes back to the turquoise.

This bracelet incorporates elaborate silverwork. These very simple fan elements may be precursors of the leaves that appeared in much of the jewelry made in the 1970s. The metals are all commercially bought, as opposed to those used in early bracelets for which the silversmith actually produced the silver sheet, pounded out the silver and pulled the wire.

JERRY DIXON
Zuni
Bracelet, 1937

2.2 x 3 x 3. Silver, turquoise. Gift of C.G. Wallace, NA-SW-ZU-J-143.

This bracelet has a baroque quality. It has time-consuming details such as the way each of the small silver balls was hammered to make a small line in the center. As with many pieces in the C.G. Wallace Collection, it is not certain whether the metalwork and lapidary work were done by the same artist or by two artists in collaboration. The person who did the metalwork drilled into a piece of railroad tie and made a half dome. He then forced these silver balls into it in order to make them the same and to line up the spacing of each of these rows.

CIPPY CRAZY HORSE
Cochiti, b. 1946
Bracelet, 2001

2.25 x 1.75 x 3.25. Silver. Heard Museum purchase from the Heard Museum Shop, 4107-1.

Cippy Crazy Horse's work recalls the early stamp work and the early row bracelets of Navajo silversmiths. But Crazy Horse is a Pueblo man, and he calls his work Pueblo stamp work. He takes great pride in the fact that his father was a silversmith. Crazy Horse makes his own silver like the early silversmiths did—he heats then pours molten silver, and then hammers and forges to create his own sheet of silver. He creates a dome in the bracelets rather than just a straight, flat bracelet.

He calls this bracelet the Michelin tire bracelet. One day on his way home from Santa Fe, he saw a woman whose car had broken down on the side of the road. He stopped to help her change a flat tire. As he changed the tire, he saw an interesting design from the tire in a puddle of mud. Thus, the Michelin tire bracelet. The genesis for an idea can really come from something as simple as that. It speaks to the history and the evolution of how people make things, and why they create things on a completely different level. For Crazy Horse, this was a completely original idea, and yet it has such great, strong links to the designs of the past.

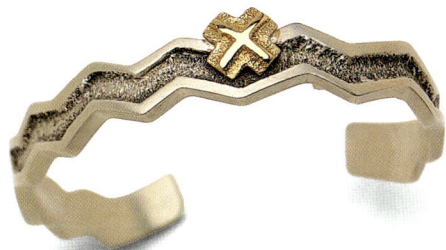

LARRY GOLSH
Pala Mission/Cherokee, b. 1943
Bracelet, 2001

1.75 x 2.5 x .66. Silver, gold. Heard Museum purchase from the Heard Museum Shop, 4107-4.

Much of Larry Golsh's jewelry was tufa cast and has a lot of textural quality. The combination of silver and gold on this bracelet is a nice statement. It also is in keeping with earlier jewelry—mixing different materials. Golsh's work is marked by an extremely modern look and simple, elegant designs in silver and gold.

RICHARD CHAVEZ
San Felipe, b. 1949
Bracelet, 1990s
2.75 x 1.25 x 2. Silver, onyx, turquoise.
Gift of Ruth and Robert Vogele, 4027-1.

Navajo bracelet, 1900-1920
1 x 2.5. Silver, turquoise. Gift in memory of Charles Faye Van Court and
Helen L. Van Court, NA-SW-NA-J-783.

This is a great example of a carved object that was incorporated into a piece of wearable silver material. The little sheep has a sweet, whimsical expression. The curvature inside the ears is great, and the nostrils and mouth are detailed.

NORBERT PESHLAKAI
Navajo, b. 1953
Bracelet, 1922
1.75 x 2.5 x 1.625. Silver, opal. Gift of
Jeanie Harlan, 3617-1.

Norbert Peshlakai's jewelry illustrates great original ideas. It is created through stamp and file work, but in a way that nobody else does. All of his work has a freshness about it. This bracelet is asymmetrical—wider on one end than on the other. The stamps are used in a random pattern, and he has set a random pattern as an outline for the bracelet. If you look closely, you will see symmetry and growth to it. It starts narrow at one end, and then flows, narrows, widens, flows, creating constant movement. He has further broken the balance by setting a single stone in a gold bezel.

HARVEY BEGAY
Navajo, b. 1938
Bracelet, 1997
2.25 x 2.5 x .75. Gold, coral. Heard Museum purchase from Faust Gallery, Scottsdale,
Arizona, 3658-1.

This tufa cast bracelet has depth. Its elegance is reminiscent of work by Harvey's father, Kenneth Begay. Coral is highly prized for its color and rarity. A really great piece of coral, especially in contemporary jewelry, entails a great deal of expense. This bracelet has an overall surface texture of tufa casting, except on the sides. He filed those away to get a contrast between the matte finish and the highly polished surfaces. The bezel also has a highly polished surface, so it dramatically sets the stone.

EDITH TSABETSAYE
Zuni, b. 1940
Bracelet, 1998

2 x 1.75 x 2.5. Sleeping Beauty turquoise, silver. Heard Museum purchase from the Heard Museum Shop, 3994-1.

Edith Tsabetsaye excels at Zuni needlepoint. The pieces that she cuts are minute, and the detailed precision with which they are put together is just outstanding. She can accomplish this because of her technical skill, and also because of the types of tools that are available.

PRESTON MONONGYE AND LEE YAZZIE
Mission/Mexican, 1927-1987 and Navajo
Bracelet, 1970s

2 x 2.4 x 1.75. Blue Gem turquoise, silver, coral. Acquired by the donor at the Heard Museum Shop in 1989. Gift of Mareen Allen Nichols, 4033-261.

This bracelet is signed inside with Preston Monongye's signature and stamp. Lee Yazzie also inlaid his initials very subtly into the design. There is one piece of coral on the side, which makes you notice the initials LAY inlaid with the same high-quality Blue Gem turquoise used in the bracelet. When C.G. Wallace was a trader, a lot of the silverwork was constructed by Navajo people, and the stonework was produced and inlaid by Zuni people. The multiple signatures on this collaborative piece are indicators of the importance that began to be given to signatures and signed pieces.

PERRY SHORTY
Navajo, b. 1964
Bracelet, 2001

2 x 2.5 x 1.125. Lone Mountain turquoise, silver. Heard Museum purchase from the artist, 4124-1.

Figures

Zuni pin, 1930s-1940s

3.5 x 2.5. Turquoise, shell, jet, coral, silver. The Fred Harvey Company probably acquired this from C.G. Wallace, who frequently sold Zuni-made material to them. Fred Harvey Fine Arts Collection, 296S and 295S.

Figures like this were made with small stands so they could be displayed when not being worn—an interesting idea. A great detail here is the piece of turquoise on one moccasin that represents a button. The other moccasin shows no button, as if the button faces outward, away from the viewer. You almost feel the figure is going to take a step because of that added little detail. Other details include the carved kilt and the hair carved into the tail of the deer.

DENISE WALLACE
Aleut, b. 1957
Boat carver pendant/pin, 1994

3.5 x 2. Silver, gold, mastedon tusk, coral, sugilite. Heard Museum purchase from Faust Gallery, Scottsdale, Arizona, 3917-1.

In this dance figure with moveable parts, Wallace draws on memories of her culture and people. Her highly personal style diverges completely from that of the Southwest, except in its reliance on cultural and spiritual figures, also characteristic of Hopi and Zuni work.

LEO POBLANO
Zuni, 1905-1959
Carved figures, 1942 and 1940s

6 x 2.2 x 1.3 and 5.75 x 2.5. Shell, turquoise, coral, jet. Gifts of Katie Noe, 3624-1 (left), and C.G. Wallace, NA-SW-ZU-F-46 (right).

There is great detail in the inlaying of the necklaces and the jewelry these figures are wearing. The man has a rolled turquoise bead necklace, and a concho belt is carved in the shell. The woman has details in her skirt that are manta pins. Behind the curve of her arm appears the back apron she is wearing. Leo Poblano used the natural curves of the shell to give movement to the figures—each appears to be stepping forward. You can see their bone structure.

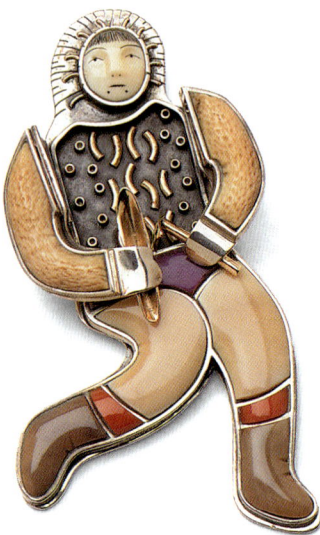

LEEKYA DEYUSE
Zuni, 1889-1966
Carved figure, 1932
1.25 x 3.25 x .5. Jet, shell, turquoise, coral. Gift of C.G.
Wallace, NA-SW-ZU-F-57.

TEDDY WEAHKEE
Zuni, 1890-1965
Inlaid figure, 1931
6.5 x 3.75. Shell, turquoise, silver, jet, spondylous shell.
Gift of C.G. Wallace, NA-SW-ZU-J-317.

*In his white shirt and all his jewelry,
this Zuni man is dressed as if he
knows his portrait is going to be
taken. The piece is a great image of
how drilling by hand was done.*

LEEKYA DEYUSE
Zuni, 1889-1966
Carved figure, 1930s
1.25 x 2 x .625. Jet, shell, turquoise, coral. Gift of C.G.
Wallace, NA-SW-ZU-F-45.

*These very carefully carved figures
represent red-winged blackbirds.
They illustrate how Indian people
reflected ideas about nature, art,
movement and space in great detail
using only simple tools.*

LEEKYA DEYUSE
Zuni, 1889-1966
Carving for pendant, 1930s
1.25 x 1.5 x .5. Turquoise, coral. Gift of C.G. Wallace, NA-SW-ZU-F-82.

*This little pendant has simplicity and is well carved. The
contrast of the colors, the softness of the green combined
with the pale coral eyes, makes it interesting.*

Necklaces + Earrings

DELLA CASA APPA
Zuni, 1889-?
Earrings, 1935

4 x 1. Silver, turquoise. Gift of C.G. Wallace, NA-SW-ZU-J-221.

This pair of Zuni inlaid earrings has a highly stylized look. At the bottom of each pendant are four tiny squash blossoms cut from very thin metal. There is a delicacy to these earrings, which are made of natural turquoise and silver.

ATTRIBUTED TO LEO POBLANO
Zuni, 1905-1959
Necklace, 1938

16.5. Silver, turquoise, jet, shell, spondylous shell. Acquired by the donor at the McCormick Auction, March 15-17, 1974. Gift of Mareen Allen Nichols, 4033-243.

DELLA CASA APPA
Zuni, 1889-?
Earrings, 1935

2.5 x 1.5. Silver, turquoise. Gift of C.G. Wallace, NA-SW-ZU-J-251.

This turquoise—as with much of the turquoise used in early jewelry—has holes drilled into each piece, an indication that each was a bead formerly used in a necklace. These earrings have movement. They are strung on wire that was hand-pulled and hand-formed, as evidenced by the changes in its diameter.

Navajo joclas, c. 1900

7. Turquoise, coral, shell. Fred Harvey Fine Arts Collection, 182BE.

This pair of joclas was probably worn both as earrings and as a pendant at the bottom of a necklace. The turquoise is natural, and there is natural discoloration through wear. They have a very nice, graceful look to them.

Santo Domingo necklace, 1940-1950

14. Shell, jet, turquoise. Acquired by the donor at Sewell's Indian Arts, Taos, New Mexico. Gift of Mareen Allen Nichols, 4033-244.

This piece is modeled after the necklaces with bird pendants that were prevalent in the Depression Era, which in turn were modeled after Hohokam mosaic pendants. The pendants are handmade, and the white shell beads are hand-drilled.

Navajo necklace, 1920-1940

14.5 x 3.5. Pink mussel shell, turquoise, silver, abalone. Gift of the Graham Foundation for Advancement in the Arts, NA-SW-NA-J-636.

This has a tied-on silver and turquoise ornament, possibly an odd earring or a piece that broke off something else. That idea of saving rather than discarding, of adding to an existing piece, gives such a necklace personal value and a new life.

Navajo necklace, c. 1900

16. Silver. Gift of the Graham Foundation for Advancement in the Arts, NA-SW-NA-J-574.

There is weight and volume to the silver beads. They were hand-polished with a steel file and, probably, steel wool or sandpaper, as evidenced by their facets. These have a wonderful squared flaring of the blossoms. The silversmith ran a steel file over the top of the bars to make the lines individually, adding a little decorative touch between the beads. The naja, or pendant, shows very heavy stamp work. The necklace is about six inches longer than contemporary ones, which was the length they were worn in the past.

Navajo necklace, c. 1930

13.75. Silver. Gift of Jacqueline Eidel, NA-SW-NA-J-737.

The squash blossoms are stylized, flatter and wider than those on earlier necklaces. They have a longer, attenuated look to them, but are still very simple. The beads are hand-polished, and each is individually made. Some of the beads on the squash blossoms are bigger than the beads on the necklace, which are more uniform. Such variations occur with individually handmade beads. In later necklaces, people began to use drills to make holes that were perfectly round. In the older necklaces, an awl was used to pierce the silver, and the resulting holes were irregular. The naja, or pendant, is complex. It has double bars of triangular wire and its ends have repoussé bumps, giving the necklace another individual touch. The piece that connects it to the necklace has stamp work on it. It is soldered to the reverse side of the naja, and then rolled to form the loop for the naja.

LEEKYA DEYUSE
Zuni, 1889-1966
Necklace, 1936

15.5 x 7.5. Spondylous shell, turquoise, coral, jet, mother of pearl. Gift of C.G. Wallace, NA-SW-ZU-J-277.

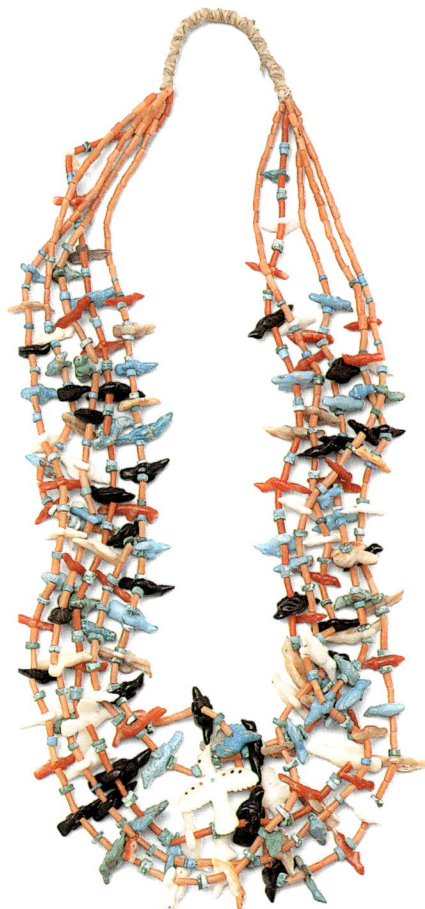

Zuni necklace, 1940

28. Blue Gem turquoise, silver, spondylous shell, jet, shell. Acquired by the donor at the McCormick Auction, March 15-17, 1974. Gift of Mareen Allen Nichols, 4033-244.

The beads are handmade and old. The holes in them have been punched out rather than drilled. While you can see the seams on some of them, they are polished. The maker took great care to make sure that the beads with seams on them were underneath the stones, rather than up at the top where they would be highly visible. When you look toward the back, these are almost all perfect. The inlay work is very intricate, very detailed, and the squash blossoms have a grace to them.

Rings + Pendants

VERMA NEQUATEWA/SONWAI
Hopi, b. 1949
Pendant, 1997
3.125 x 1. Gold, coral, sugilite, turquoise, opal. Heard Museum purchase from the artist, 3654-1.

This double-sided pendant can be worn on either side. The bale, or pendant loop, is balanced and nicely formed—an architectural statement. The surface cast has little holes in it that Verma Nequatewa made into an asset by inlaying the pendant with a multitude of stones. This is very reminiscent of jewelry that Nequatewa's uncle, Charles Loloma, made in the 1980s. His gold cuff bracelets had the surface texture of tufa casting on them. Although they looked like solid gold bracelets, they had little openings like this on the side, and you could see through to the color of the stone. When you turned it around, you would see that the entire inside of the bracelet was inlaid. He developed the idea of a piece as something to be shown to the outside world, yet also with a private aspect known only to the individual wearer. Inside the striking gold bracelet was wonderful detail. This pendant is a legacy and an extension of Loloma's idea.

Zuni ring, early 1900s
1 x 1.12. Silver, turquoise, jet, spondylous shell, shell. Fred Harvey Fine Arts Collection, 895S.

This has extreme boldness, but it also carries a soft, fluid look. The design ideas are not just from the Southwest, but are universal.

Navajo ring, late 1800s

, Silver, garnet. Fred Harvey Fine Arts Collection, 92S.

The top part of the ring is a tufa ast blank. The lines and little balls vere carved out with files. The ilversmith created volume out of a lat piece of silver by rounding it, reating the look and richness of nore material.

ncestral Pueblo rings, pre-contact

'88. Jet. Fred Harvey Fine Arts Collection, 1073S nd 1074S.

Rings like these were made with ery simple tools before Spanish ontact. Similar rings with these ame designs would have been nade out of shells, wood, whatever vas available prior to silver.

MORRIS ROBINSON
Hopi, 1900-1987
Rings, 1940s-1950s

1.5 x .75 and 1.875 x 1. Silver. Heard Museum purchase from Mary Margaret Schimfessel, who was employed by Fred Wilson, 3706-2 and 3706-1.

These two rings are finely crafted using repoussé, appliqué and stamping. Though by the same maker, each has a distinct look. The first is heavily stamped, yet the result is a simple, pleasing design. The other has a very clean, fluid, contemporary look. It also has repoussé, but instead of the repoussé dividing it into equal parts, it's divided at an angle. Morris Robinson created volume on a flat plane by using only hand tools rather than casting to make curves.

MONICA KING
Pima/Tohono O'odham/Navajo, b. 1959
Ring, 1999

1.5 x 2 x 5. Silver. Gift of the artist, 4034-1.

Monica King's work is distinctive. A well-taught artist with technological skills, King's work is completely different from that of other jewelers. There is a sense of whimsy, and also of the structural realities of how things are. The parts that move, the parts that grow away from the pieces, are what are so important about this ring. She has created many series involving mechanical parts and moving parts. On this ring, the wheels move, and you can see the spiral. You wonder what functioning mechanism she was thinking about when she put this together. It would appeal to a person who is interested in tools and machinery. For an interesting object, or one that has depth, this is the piece.

Belts + Bolos

Navajo belt, c. 1900

45.3. Silver, leather. Gift of Mareen Allen Nichols, 4033-234.

Navajo belt, c. 1940

40.5 x 2.5. Silver, leather. Fred Harvey Fine Arts Collection, 251S.

This belt has good stamp work, and the diamond center is reminiscent of the diamond slot of early belts. The buckle is tufa cast and badly weathered, but it is very bold—it shows the importance that buckles can have on these belts. This silversmith was good at casting but probably did not have quality tools to finish the piece well. It must be seen in the context of tools and working conditions of the time. Creative effort and the interplay of ideas are what make a piece important or good, and this belt takes older ideas from the past and interprets them in a smaller and more wearable form, which was also more salable. Salability is a factor in the development of this art form. When the first tourists stepped off the train, things started changing immediately; this is an indication of how things changed.

FRANK VACIT
Zuni, b. 1915
Belt, 1948

26 x 1.16. Silver, turquoise, coral, jet, shell. Acquired by the donor at the McCormick Auction, March 15-17, 1974. Gift of Mareen Allen Nichols, 4033-240.

This is a simple, sophisticated link belt that is a very stylized and angular form of a parrot design.

RODERICK TENORIO
Santo Domingo, b. 1955
Bolo tie, 1994

23.75 x 3. Number 8 turquoise, silver, leather. Purchased by the donors at the Heard Museum Guild Indian Fair & Market. Gift of Richard and Lois Rogers, 4028-1.

Tenorio interprets nature stylistically. The trumpets of the flowers open and the hummingbird's beak moves toward them. Most bolo tips match at the bottom, but Tenorio continues the hummingbird design for the bolo tips in this piece with its highly complex stamping. Viewers see the connection of ideas, but also the separation between them. Here an individual craftsman emerges as an artist.

Navajo belt, 1890

42 x 3.75. Silver, leather. Gift of the Graham Foundation for Advanced Studies in the Arts, NA-SW-NA-J-522.

This large belt, with its massive use of silver and dramatic conchos, combines complexity and simplicity. The belt's center resembles the punch hole of the diamond slot in earlier belts, but it is a raised center made by using the repoussé technique rather than being cut out. The very elaborate stamp work focuses your eye on that central part of the concho, which is further emphasized by a break in the stamp work, making your eye pause one more time before it moves to the center or to the edge.

The buckle is the best part of this belt. It is tufa cast silver that was later stamped. The very wide ridges are stamped on top to draw attention to the space. The buckle has depth, dimension. There are lines of elaborate stamp work on top of the disks, and then smooth lines again, and then top stamped ridges of lines. The square opening for the buckle also is stamped with very fine lines.

Loloma

CHARLES LOLOMA
Hopi, 1921-1991
Bracelet, 1975

3.25 x 2.5 x .8. Gold, lapis lazuli, turquoise, coral. Acquired by the donor at Ashton Gallery, Scottsdale, Arizona. Gift of Mareen Allen Nichols, 4033-246A.

This is an example of the mesa outlines visible in Charles Loloma's jewelry. From the side, you see ridges of lapis and coral and turquoise rising out of the flat area of the gold as well as bits of gold bars mixed with the stones. Singular pieces of stone are cut rather than using a massive blue or a solid color. Loloma carefully juxtaposed stones side by side so that each one has a different surface quality and a different surface color. There is a great sense of color and texture in all of his work.

CHARLES LOLOMA
Hopi, 1921-1991
Naja, 1950s

2.63 x 2. Silver. Heard Museum purchase from Bahti Indian Arts, Tucson, Arizona, NA-SW-HO-J-101.

CHARLES LOLOMA
Hopi, 1921-1991
Bowguard, 1968

3.5 x 3.5. Silver, leather, turquoise, coral. Heard Museum purchase from Bahti Indian Arts, Tucson, Arizona, NA-SW-HO-J-99.

This bowguard is made by tufa casting, leaving one side rough and the other smooth. There is a prominent hole on the smooth side, and a band of turquoise and coral—all different colors and levels—is inlaid in it. Loloma's work first appears to be contemporary and avant garde. But at the heart of this man, he is Hopi. In so much of his work, you see the land, you see katsina faces. You can see the symbolism here of the contrast between light and dark, land and space, his religion. But they are very simple understated statements.

One of the interesting things about his early work, and the work of most other jewelers, is that Loloma used available materials. Most jewelers try to work with the best materials they can afford. In a lot of the early Loloma pieces, the turquoise is not as good as stones he would later use. But still, each stone was chosen with great care in regard to color. The contrast in color and materials are important to his pieces; he wasn't afraid to take risks. The result is an interesting play between the colors. He had an amazing sense of color.

CHARLES LOLOMA
Hopi, 1921-1991
Bracelet, 1975-1980

2.25 x 3.375 x 1.6. Silver, ironwood, coral, turquoise, lapis lazuli, ivory, mastedon tusk. Gift of Barbara Haas in memory of Alvin Hass, 3662-2.

The linear qualities of the design are important. There are lines that grow, but at angles. Interspersed in those angles are tiny pieces of square-cut stones that give it dimension. The stones in this bracelet closely follow the curve of the silver. In later years, in later work, the stones project dramatically away from the surface of Loloma's work.

CHARLES LOLOMA
Hopi, 1921-1991
Bolo tie, 1950s

18 x 2.25. Silver, leather. Heard Museum purchase from Bahti Indian Arts, Tucson, Arizona, NA-SW-HO-J-97.

This ram's head bolo tie is a very simple tufa cast piece with stamp and file work. Smooth surfaces contrast with very heavy sand cast texture. The texture in the face and along the ears really gives this piece depth, gives it character. It might be worn by someone who might not be from the West or would never consider wearing a bolo tie.

CHARLES LOLOMA
Hopi, 1921-1991
Ring, 1975

1.6 x 1. Gold, lapis lazuli, turquoise, coral. Acquired by the donor at Ashton Gallery, Scottsdale, Arizona. Gift of Mareen Allen Nichols, 4033-246B.

In the 1970s, Charles Loloma was working with abstract shapes. His jewelry began to grow in depth and in height. The stones in this ring go all the way around the surface creating a very dramatic effect. Loloma pieces are wonderfully finished on the inside so that there is a smoothness to them and a comfort for the wearer.

C O L L E C T I N G

B E A D W O R K   A N D   J E W E L R Y

DIANA F. PARDUE

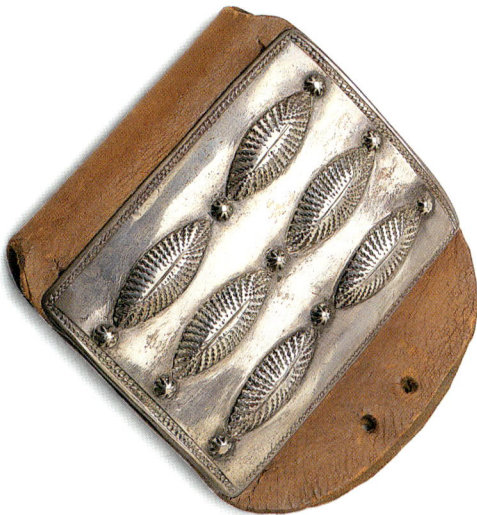

Navajo bowguard, c. 1900

3.75 x 3.4 x 1. Silver, leather. This bowguard is visible in a 1910 photograph of Dwight and Maie Heard's home (facing page). Both bowguards and the concho belt seen in the photograph are in the Heard Museum Collection today. Heard Museum Collection, NA-SW-NA-J-26.

This bold, simple and classic bowguard has beautiful stamp work. An early piece, it was made before the use of stones. The flat surface is given volume through the design elements and repoussé. —GAIL BIRD AND YAZZIE JOHNSON

AFTER MAIE AND DWIGHT HEARD moved to Phoenix in 1895, they began collecting and displaying Native arts in their home and in Dwight Heard's office. Jewelry and beadwork appear sparingly in photographs of their showcase home, Casa Blanca, that was decorated predominately with baskets and textiles. A 1910 photograph taken by Dwight Heard's cousin, Fred Bancroft (facing page), reveals two silver bowguards and one concho belt hanging on a wall in one room of the home.

In the course of her lifetime, Maie Heard acquired approximately 75 items of silver jewelry that were added to the collection of the museum. As with other purchases made by the Heards, few records exist to document any acquisitions prior to 1927. At that time, the Heards' private collection had grown. They were planning the museum and began retaining sales receipts. The few existing records of jewelry purchases are from local shops such as Graves Indian Shop and Anna Fullen's shop at the San Carlos Hotel in Chandler, Arizona. Several items of jewelry including rings, earrings and a bracelet were purchased by Maie Heard in 1930 from the Fred Harvey Company's main showroom and sales shop at the Alvarado Hotel in Albuquerque, New Mexico. Prior to that purchasing trip, Maie Heard wrote to the Harvey Company indicating a desire to purchase items for the museum.

The first curator of the museum, Allie Walling BraMé, acquired jewelry for the Heard and also sold pieces to the museum from her private collection. BraMé and her husband at that time, Herbert, had helped the museum acquire a wide range of cultural materials during the two years prior to its opening.

Several important jewelry collections have been donated to the museum in more recent years. In 1975, Zuni trader C.G. Wallace donated a 500-object jewelry collection in conjunction with a landmark auction of his collection in Phoenix by Sotheby's. As a trader, Wallace had amassed a remarkable collection that included works by outstanding artists such as Leekya Deyuse, Leo Poblano and Teddy Weahkee. The collection is strong in important major works by these artists and others, but an additional strength is that it was well-documented by Wallace as to maker and date. It includes important jewelry made mainly from 1920 through the 1940s. Some of the earliest Wallace pieces at the Heard that were made for sale are carvings by Leekya Deyuse and Teddy Weahkee, from the late 1920s. These and similar works document the development of the Zuni early figurative carving style created as single figures and as necklace pendants. These forms are complemented in the Wallace Collection by carved works set in silver as well as significant examples of mosaic and inlay.

In 1978, the Fred Harvey Foundation donated a 4,000-object collection to the museum, approximately 1,000 objects of which were silver jewelry. The fascinating aspect of the Harvey Company jewelry collection is its diversity and range. There were definite efforts, probably on the part of the main buyer for the Harvey Company, Herman Schweizer, to collect objects that documented changes of one object type over several decades and to purchase unique items. Schweizer's favorite item among the thousands in the Harvey Company Collection and during his more than 40 years of building the collection was an Ancestral Pueblo necklace from Pueblo Bonito (page 47).

The Harvey Company is popularly remembered now for lightweight tourist jewelry it sold in the 1930s. Many of these less expensive items were mass produced and sold to the Harvey Company by the H.H. Tammen Company in Denver, Colorado. The collection of jewelry that was retained, however, represents high-quality works that were also sold by the Harvey Company. Many were made from coin silver in unique designs set with superb turquoise stones.

Another important collection was donated to the museum in 1983 by the Graham Foundation for Advanced Studies in the Arts. More than 200 items of jewelry, mostly Navajo-made and many from the turn of the century, comprise this collection.

The Navajo, Zuni and Pueblo jewelry from the late 1800s through the first half of the 20th century in the C.G. Wallace Collection, the Fred Harvey Fine Arts Collection and the Graham Foundation Collection were complemented in 1999 through a donation by Heard life trustee Mareen Allen Nichols. She began her collection after she moved with her husband, Dr. Dean Nichols, to Phoenix in the late 1950s, and she continued to add to it through the 1980s. The Nichols Collection contains 267 examples of important early works, but consists primarily of jewelry of top-quality craftsmanship from the 1960s and 1970s with an emphasis on a diversity of turquoise stones. A wide range of works by ground-breaking artists such as Charles Loloma, Hopi, and Preston Monongye, Mission/Mexican, are featured. According to guest curators Gail Bird, Santo Domingo/Laguna, and Yazzie Johnson, Navajo, the Nichols Collection completed the museum's collection by bringing it into the present.

The beadwork collections at the museum share a somewhat similar history to that of the jewelry. Maie and Dwight Heard purchased Plains beadwork from Herbert and Allie Walling BraMé, the couple hired to acquire objects for the museum when it was in the planning stages in 1927 and 1928. The BraMés secured important Northern Plains beaded items including a Sioux cradleboard and saddlebags.

Cutnose and wife,
Northern Cheyenne,
hold a beaded tobacco
bag, c. 1875. Photograph
by Cosand & Mosser.
Trustrim Connell
Photography Collection,
Heard Museum, RC
5(2):36.

The beadwork collections have been augmented throughout the museum's more than seventy-year history. Additional beadwork items were donated to the museum by Maie Heard's sister, Florence Dibbell Bartlett, who eventually founded the Museum of International Folk Art in Santa Fe, New Mexico. Among Bartlett's donations are a Kiowa child's beaded buckskin outfit of pants, shirt and moccasins and a MacKenzie River beaded velvet baby carrier (page 11). The first major gift to the museum of Plains material was a collection of 20 items donated in 1945 by Mrs. Edward Manville. The collection had been developed from 1939 to 1945 while the Manvilles lived among the Blackfeet people in Montana.

As with other collections formed by the Fred Harvey Company, those items from the Plains are of particular importance. The Harvey Company purchased large collections from private individuals or from estates focusing on items made west of Mississippi. Although the Harvey Company maintained a showroom and sales room in Albuquerque, they did set aside collections for a display room, known locally as a museum, at the onset. By 1904, the Harvey Company was attempting to sell portions of the "museum collection" to large natural history museums and developed descriptive catalogues of the collections available. George A. Dorsey, who took a sixteen-month leave of absence from the Field Museum in Chicago from 1903 to 1904 to work for the Harvey Company, appears to have been instrumental in developing these catalogues as well as writing a popular book for travelers west via the Santa Fe Railway.

The collections listed in the catalogue pages were organized according to tribal affiliation, and each object was identified and described. Some entries were written by Dorsey's colleagues, who were acquiring collections for both the Field Museum and the Harvey Company in 1903 and 1904. For example, the descriptions for the Pomo material from California were provided by John Hudson, who had also sold Pomo and Hupa collections to the Harvey Company and the Field Museum. Dorsey probably wrote the descriptions for the majority of the Plains collections, possibly relying on information from another curator at the Field Museum, S. Chapman Simms, for the Crow material. The Harvey Company was successful in selling some Plains collections such as the one of Crow material to the Museum de Volkerkunde in Berlin, Germany, in 1905. Collections of Arapaho, Cheyenne, Crow, Osage and Mandan objects were sold to the Carnegie Museum of Natural History in Pittsburgh in 1904. Part of the Kiowa collection described in 1904 catalogue records developed by Dorsey was not sold, but included in the 1978 donation to the Heard.

A collection of 300 objects, many of which are beaded, was donated to the Heard in 1956 by Mrs. John C. Lincoln. This collection consisted mainly of Woodlands and Plains material and broadened the museum's scope in those areas, making this a major step in the development of a depth of material outside the Southwest. Curator Tom Cain wrote in his monthly report for March 1956, "During the month the museum was the recipient of the largest single gift of museum items in the past five years. Through the generosity of Mrs. John C. Lincoln we now have over three hundred items of American Indian culture . . . we are especially pleased at the range and quality of the material."

Collections of Woodlands beaded materials given to the Heard were further strengthened by donations of Byron Harvey III, the great-grandson of Fred Harvey. Byron Harvey's association with the Heard was formalized in the late 1960s, when the Fred Harvey Company collection was loaned to the museum. His first major gift to the Heard was in 1971. Through the years, his donations totaled more than 2,000 objects, with many items coming from the Southwest, Plains and Woodlands.

In 1983, the museum received from the estate of Carolann Smurthwaite a collection of Cheyenne beaded items and Kiowa ledgers as well as 170 photographic prints taken primarily in Oklahoma Territory in the 1870s and 1880s. The collection was formed by Smurthwaite's grandfather, Trustrim Connell, who served in the 138th Pennsylvania

Southern Cheyenne or Southern Arapaho moccasins, late 1800s

11 x 4.5 x 4.5. Deer hide, buffalo hide, glass beads, sinew. Estate of Carolann Smurthwaite, NA-PL-CH-C-24A, B.

These are excellent due to the choice of colors, balance of design, the use of cut beads and the use of small beads.

——MAYNARD WHITE OWL LAVADOUR

Infantry during the Civil War where, in 1865, he was awarded the Congressional Medal of Honor. Connell continued in military service and after his marriage in 1867, he was moved to Indian Territory in present-day Oklahoma. Connell, his wife Annie and daughter Caroline moved to Phoenix in 1898. Caroline Connell married Charles Frederick Smurthwaite in 1907, and daughter Carolann was born in 1918. Carolann became an active member of the Heard Museum Guild, and she owned and operated an antique shop begun in 1929 by her mother at the Arizona Biltmore Resort. Among her other items that came to the museum were two brooches by Kenneth Begay, Navajo (pages 4 and 49).

The collections of jewelry and beadwork so enthusiastically begun by Maie and Dwight Heard 100 years ago, have continued to grow through the years through the contributions of generous donors as well as a small number of purchases.